Money Master's Guide

Game Mastering For Fun And Profit

By Raymond J. Hicks

ARJADE PRODUCTIONS

Legal:

Cover art by William McAusland
Edited by Luke Swadling
Layout by Alan Tucker

ISBN: 978-0-6483210-7-1

Published by Arjade Productions, Mittagong 2022

This book is not written by a financial advisor. The details given on the following pages are a recount of philosophies regarding how I constructed my business and should not be taken as advice for your own situation. Every individual's circumstances are different and you should always consult a financial professional before making any life decisions that may impact your financial state. As you read on you will see that many of my ideas failed and as a result I learnt the lessons distilled into this book.

Dedication:
I am lucky enough to have two absolute girlbosses in my life who encourage me to pursue the hustle and make my mark. This book is dedicated to them.

To my mother Kath who taught me the importance of life balance, working hard, and not taking crap from anyone as a business strategy.

To my executive level, breadwinning wife, Rachel, for her endless support and always being my number one fan. May Rhynessa and Phelthorn adventure together forever.

Acknowledgments
This book would not exist without two very important people; Pete "Shotgun" Shanahan who has kept me sane through some very not sane times, and Luke "van Dorne" Swadling whose work ethic and willingness to help makes me want to be a better and more hardworking creator. Thank you both beyond measure.

I also have to acknowledge all the friends who helped me with my silly ideas of all kinds over the years, particularly this book. Those who rode with me as I made many stupid mistakes and learnt my lessons. Finally, thank you to those who helped me back up after each and every fall.

Table of Contents

Prologue - A Job Offer 5
Introduction - The Sage Mentor 7
Chapter 1 - Imagination to Currency Conversion Machine. 10
Imagination, Question Mark, Profit - A Simple Equation 10
Knowing Your Audience 15
Scope and Perfection - King vs Martin 18
Chapter 2 - Building a Community 20
Consistent and Authentic Engagement 21
The Rest of the Book. 26
Chapter 3 - Adventures in Writing. 28
Writing Adventures 28
Selling Adventures 29
Chapter 4 - Running Games. 33
Setting Expectations and Using Safety Tools 33
Running for Shops 38
Running for Conventions. 43
Running as a Special Event 47
Running as a Service. 52
Chapter 5 - Streaming/Podcasting Games 58
Performers vs Your Friends 59
Legal Concerns 62
Growing Audiences 66
A Realistic Expectation 71
Chapter 6 - Blogging/Podcasting Content 73
Regularity of Content 73
Chapter 7 - Chasing the Social Media Dragon. 79
Growing a Following 79
Where's the Money, Lebowski? 82
Chapter 8 - Conventions. 86
Who Gets Chosen to Run 86
What Gets to Run 88
Volunteering and Converting to Sales 89
Selling at a Booth. 91
Chapter 9 - Crowdfunding 96
How Kickstarter/Crowdfunding Works. 96
No Crowd, No Fund. 99
Fulfilment Breaks the Bank. 100
Money Now, Product Now. 102
Chapter 10 - Fiction Writing 105
Storytelling vs Fiction Writing. 106
Editing is Key 108
Marketing. 111
Chapter 11 - Content Writing and Copywriting. 113
Writing is Writing 113
Out of the Box. 116
Diversity of Product 117
Chapter 12 - Products Multiplied by Time Equals Profit. 119
Your Biggest Ally. 119
Building a Catalogue. 120
Passive Income 121
Having Fun 122
Conclusion 123

Prologue - A Job Offer

I knew what I was doing was technically illegal, but I couldn't help myself. I sat there with a massive smile on my face. How was I getting away with this? I couldn't believe it. I felt all giddy, like before a first date or in the car ride home after buying a brand new treat for myself that I couldn't wait to dig into. It was euphoric. It was ecstatic. I had finally done it! I couldn't believe it. I hadn't felt this good in a long time and I was high on the thrill of it. And then I heard the siren. I was busted. But even that couldn't take away the smirk from my face. I knew that this was only the beginning.

Now that's a pretty exciting start to a story, right? I bet that isn't what you had in mind when you purchased this book. Now you might be sitting there hooked on the thrill of it all and wanting to know the rest of the drama that is about to unfold, or you could also be sitting there asking yourself if the rest of this book is about to advocate embezzling money or breaking the law. You can rest assured it is not, nor is it even a particularly dramatic moment in my life story. But as you can plainly see, we game masters have a gift for constructing narrative that is exciting and engaging. And that is a skill that is always in demand.

I am so confident in your ability to also do this, that right now before we even start our journey, I am going to offer you a paying job of sorts. If you are reading this and want to put your Game Mastering skills to work for you, send me an email at mail@arjade.net and we can find you a project to work on. We can work out exactly what that is going to entail once I hear from you. But I am always looking for help and I would love to extend that opportunity to you as I have hundreds of others already.

Don't worry, the breaking of the law I was doing was simply using my phone whilst driving. You see, I had just been emailed my first paycheck for running a game of dungeons and dragons. It was the first time my ABN (Australian Business Number, for those unfamiliar) had actually been used to accrue income. I was giddy with excitement and couldn't put my phone down as I undertook the two hour drive back to my home. I got caught looking at the phone whilst at a red light and the police officer issued me a small ticket for a minor infraction. But I didn't care because the money I just got paid was more than double what the ticket was worth.

There is no better feeling than being paid for something that you have been previously doing for fun. Especially if doing that comes naturally to you. In this book I would like to share with you my story of how I am turning my Game Mastering hobby into solid gold so that you too can do the same. We are going to look at a wide range of methods that Game Masters around the world are currently doing to make money from their hobby. I am going to talk about the ups and downs, the risks and rewards, and hopefully inspire you to look into your own situation and identify opportunities for you to do the same.

Please keep in mind that it may not work out, and this isn't advice directly for you to take. Make sure you treat anything in this book with careful consideration and assess your own financial situation with a professional accountant or financial advisor. There are MANY things that I am going to be detailing in this book that simply did not work for me and did not make me money. So be warned, not every financial situation is the same and you should make educated decisions with the help of experienced professionals.

Introduction - The Sage Mentor

Okay, so who am I and why should you listen to me? For those who don't know who I am, allow me to introduce myself. Hi! My name is Raymond J. Hicks and I have been a big fan of tabletop roleplaying games for over two decades. For the past 12 years (at least at the time of writing this book) I have been using my hobby to make money for myself as a side hustle. Over those years I have found many ways to articulate the skill set that is required for Game Mastering into cash.

My first adventure module has sold over 2,000 copies world wide and as I write this I have just finished my work for a successful Kickstarter in collaboration with Crit Academy with over 350 backers, granting us over 18,000 (Australian) dollars to get that book made, printed and distributed. I have been paid as a game master for over a decade and have run games at conventions, for shops, for community groups and even privately. Through my games I have managed to aggregate a very large campaign setting and an abundance of highly detailed fiction stories which are slated for print in the coming year. Every day I post for the Game Master Stash, a social media page which has grown from less than 1,000 followers when I started with them several years ago, all the way up to 17,000+ followers today.

I am also the founder of Arjade Productions, a publishing company that has slowly been growing and finding its feet for over a decade. My goal for this production company is to offer undiscovered and talented writers a path to publish their works and to build their portfolios in a way that gives them a stepping stone into the industry.

I believe that our community grows strongest when we all help each other to achieve our goals. With that in mind, I have been having great success in the last few years and wanted to share with you all the different ways I have been making my hobby work for me.

I want this book to be an honest conversation between you and myself. I am not here to give you step by step guides for how to do everything in this book, but I am here to share with you my advice and experiences. Everything in this book is something I have tried myself in the past. Where some endeavours have been successful, others have not been as big a win as I would have liked. With that in mind every single idea here has taught me a lesson about business and how to make money with gaming.

Why am I not giving tutorials of how to do things, you may ask? Well aside from the significant length that would add to an already lengthy project the fact of the matter is that in today's age of constantly innovating technologies the processes by which I do things are constantly changing. Even between when I first started writing this book and now in the final editing stages the methods I use to write and promote and make content have changed. If I were to detail specific actions to take, by the time you read this in the future those actions may be irrelevant or even no longer possible. The best thing for you to do is find the tutorials that are most recent and relevant during the time you are ready to take action. Me writing down what I do will get old and outdated very swiftly.

I also want to set a realistic expectation for you. This **isn't** a get-rich-quick scheme. Don't quit your day job right now and pursue a life of game content creation, because at the end of the day, those bills are gonna come knocking on your door. Whilst some avenues discussed here are more profitable than others, everything we talk about together in this book will require some investment of time. The dividends of that work may take time to find their way back to you.

With the exception of streaming/podcasting and social media influencing it is unlikely you are going to make a livable income off any single one of these ideas. But with a little effort, some time under your belt, and some creativity and determination you will begin to turn the fun stuff you currently do for free into small opportunities to grow your wealth. If you are lucky and patient, over time that could be a seed you can use to grow a following and develop into something more. But I wanted to start here from the outset with an honest comment to set realistic goals.

It is absolutely okay for your journey to take a long time to get somewhere truly profitable. The beauty with many of these ideas we are going to discuss is that they are like a snowball rolling down a mountain. You start off small, one book here, one resource there, and sure those two things make you $20 in their first month. But they also make you $20 in your second month. And maybe the third month they only make you $5. But then at some point four years down the track from now they are still making you $15 here and $10 there, along with the dozens of other things that you have put out into the world; And the beauty of that is that it is 100% Passive income, You just have to remember to click the "collect royalties" button when you need a payout.

All that being said, I guarantee you there is something in this book you haven't considered and I hope you can learn from the things I have to say. You don't have to pursue every idea presented in every chapter of this book. Feel free to skip the ones you aren't interested in. Please be sure to start with chapter 1, and take a read of chapter 12 regardless of your plans. Everything else is up to you.

I really look forward to hearing your success stories and seeing your work contributing to our amazing community.

Chapter 1 - Imagination to Currency Conversion Machine

Let's imagine you are in any industry. For the sake of this experiment, let us say you are a farmer. You grow up learning about animals and crops and land and the day finally comes for you to use that knowledge to make a fortune. What is required of you to get started? Maybe you need some land, and some seeds. You have to prepare the soil. Maybe you need some livestock. Maybe you need good weather and some possibly expensive equipment. Getting started as a farmer takes a lot of effort and resources before you can really get going. The same is true for most industries; retail, hospitality, craftsmanship, or a trade.

One of the best things about using your game mastering skills is that a great deal of the "raw" resources you will be using is just your creativity and your time. You don't really need anything fancy to get started. Heck, right this minute as I write this I am sitting in bed on my phone typing this whilst I try to relax enough to get sleepy. You won't believe how much of my creative work gets done on a bathroom break or in waiting rooms or in boring meetings.

All you need to work as a game master is your imagination and some time, and depending on your chosen pathway a bit of technology to write with or make things. Anyone can do it. I assume you purchased this book with some technology, maybe you are even reading it on your phone or tablet. That is all you need.

You are an imagination machine. All that is missing is finding a way to connect that imagination generator to a currency converter.

Imagination, Question Mark, Profit - A Simple Equation

Before we start talking "strategy" for building your product base, we first have to talk about two things. First off, the mindset we will need to do this successfully, and secondly a brief discussion about building a fan base. Whatever your path that you plan to take, its success or failure is going to most likely stem from the kind of fanbase you cultivate. So these first two chapters are going to dig into that a little more. This is our process. It's not just making products and then making cash. The good news is you can start working on both your mindset and your fanbase with zero products.

Let's start with your mindset. Making money is a fairly straightforward process. Make something and sell it for more than it cost to make. Depending on how you value your time and energy, creating something sellable with nothing but your imagination is fairly cheap. This makes it perfect as a raw resource to exploit for capitalist gain. You already own the means for production of this content; your mind and a machine to type and distribute your content.

With everything business related, it is important to consider your COSTS vs REVENUE. A big mistake many people make is buying hundreds of dollars of stock art for a book that makes them less than a hundred dollars. Always keep in mind the cost of what you are doing. Another common mistake I see regularly is people paying more for advertising than they receive back on investment. Keep this in mind when you are at the final stages of getting your work out there.

You MUST cover the cost of whatever you are making. There is little point in making a product and losing money on its sale. That is just backwards thinking. There are some instances where this is absolutely vital and we will talk about them as we come across them. Don't fall for that trap.

Personally I like to see each individual project as a stepping stone, particularly when you are starting out. Let's say you do an adventure module that needs Goblin artwork. Buying that art is a small expense that you have to factor into the cost of the project. Include that in your price, but the upside is that now you have goblin artwork and you can use that for the future.

This can actually be a useful way of planning what projects to do next. If you pick projects that add to your portfolio of assets you will grow the pool of what is available in future. That means the cost to make your next project is cheaper because of smart planning and more of the price you sell it for goes back into your pocket.

Finding the right price for your work is something you have to do for yourself. There is a delicate balance between charging so little that you don't make money, and charging so much you scare off customers. I have often worked with artists and writers who set their price at a point that was out of my reach. I had one lady I was working with who would charge me $150US per painting. In Australian Dollars that often meant I could only get one art work on special occasions. I would go years between buying artworks. Had she priced her work at $80US, I could have afforded it more regularly and would have bought art once every month or two. Instead of making 6-12 sales at $80 each year (between $480-720US) she was lucky to get a single sale (often $0US per year). I often wont buy a module or novel for $25 but will happily buy 5 for $10 each. You and I both know that this doesn't make any rational sense and logic dictates I shouldn't do this. But humans are not driven by logic, they are driven by emotions and being bad at maths. At the end of the day you do have to work this out for yourself but my attitude is to keep your barriers to entry as low as possible for your customers, and price is often a big one; if not the biggest.

A final word on price. If you offer something for free people will take it. In my experience it rarely translates to additional sales or marketing. When I first started I offered my adventure module "Saraahd's Secret Shrine" as a digital title under "pay what you want," meaning that people could pay any amount they chose. Almost always they chose zero. It is still available under the same system and you can grab it for free right now if you wanted. But very few people have then gone on to actually spend money on my work because of that. It is a great module and I have received many comments from people who ran the scenario and absolutely loved it. I am also very proud of the additional world building content that is in that module. People who download/buy it and run it, love it. But my other products haven't then gone on to have a bump in sales as a result of such positive feedback. So be warned.

This also works for social media and promotions. In the past I have run give-aways and done follower trains for zero net benefit to myself. Every day I post for free on Game Master Stash on Facebook. From time to time I try to use that as a platform to get the word out about my products, but very rarely do I see that translate into more than 100 sales despite having 17,000+ followers who regularly see and engage with our content. So don't say I didn't warn you. Make sure you charge for your hard work if you would like to get paid for it.

Many Roads to Treasure

Let's talk about fanbase. There are many roads to be taken. We are going to look at several of them, but these are not the only way. If you have an idea, then by all means try it out. The only reason I have enough advice to fill a book is because I tried so many different things.

We live in a time where publishing content is entirely democratised. Anyone with a small investment of time and energy can self publish novels, games or even a whole range of previously unobtainable things. Even within a single sub-category, like publishing games content, there are a plethora of different ways to accomplish that. This is something that I have witnessed change in my own lifetime.

I am a fan of the musician and performance artist Amanda Palmer. When I first started following her the only way to get your music out to people was through a big record company. A few years after I began following her she entered a lawsuit to break her contract with her record label and was successful. This meant she was all on her own, and whatever chances she took would require her engaging with her own followers. In many interviews she has talked about how "to a record company (or big publisher for us writers) making 25,000 sales just isn't enough. But for an artist with 25,000 loyal and devoted fans that is a dream come true. You can live off that kind of a following." You can support a community that size and get support back in return. To a big corporation that is nothing, but to an artist that is everything. You are an artist and what you are trying to build is community-focussed in its nature. This is a good thing, and this advice shows us how the world has changed today.

I tell you that story because that thought is what I come back to whenever I feel down about not making progress. In time, your audience grows. And as you see those names and emails coming back again and again for future projects you start to feel the love that exists in your tribe. We are going to talk more about building that community and finding your own tribe in the next chapter. You are no longer bound by the gatekeepers and the metrics measuring how "successful" you are. It is just you, a keyboard, and your fans.

These days you do not have to go through a big corporation to reach an audience. In fact more and more people my age and younger are tuning out from mass produced content and focusing in on those creators that actually make connections with us. It has never been a better time to be a creator than now as so many options are already on the table. People are also very open to new options these days. There are no rules for finding your audience and you can use any means necessary to accomplish that.

Writing, publishing, self publishing, vlogging, blogging, streaming, podcasting or just being really engaged on reddit or twitter can all be ways to get your name out there. Whatever you are drawn to, you can do it and make it work for you. The trick is then finding ways to turn that pathway into a lucrative one. Once you find your distribution medium and start finding your tribe, the next step is to start learning their customs and rituals.

The Toll Collector and the Fuzz

No book about self run business would be complete without a caveat about taxes and copyright law. Every person's situation is different. Depending on what you are planning to do, where you live, how much money you make, what social security you are entitled for, etc. you may find yourself in some legal hot mess.

It is important that whatever path you take you are proactive in doing the research for what legal and taxation requirements exist for you. If you are selling things internationally you may need to apply for tax permits. If you are running events for young people you may need to do a working with children check. Do you need public liability insurance? All of these questions are vital to know ahead of time.

Doing a bit of research is going to save you a lot of stress in the long run. My advice for dealing with this is to find someone who is doing what you want to be doing, and speak to them about what you need to know to get started. When I published my first adventure module I spent 3 hours talking to a small independent game publisher about what I needed to know. It is hard to find answers to these questions because you don't know the things that you haven't encountered yet. You can't prepare questions about areas of ignorance. Your best bet is to speak to people who have been there and done that. The last thing you want is to be thrown in jail for tax evasion.

Knowing Your Audience

As an admin at the Game Master Stash I have seen a lot of content come through our page. I have also seen many admins come and go. There is often a temptation to create these huge, larger than life NPCs or these big complicated backstories for dungeons and adventures. Often many admins get frustrated with how long it takes them to produce content with such depth and complexity. What usually happens to such content is that it does not do well. Which in turn becomes frustrating to see all your hard work go unappreciated.

Knowing what content sells helps both you and your audience. Generic, easy to use stuff always outperforms specific overly complicated topics. The same is true for making game content.

Think about it. Why is your audience coming to you in the first place? Do they want an intricate story with various political ins and outs to keep track of, a new system added into the game, various NPCs who aren't what they say they are with a confusing plot that twists and turns? Or do they want a simple dungeon crawl to run because they need to fill in some sessions whilst they are busy and don't have time to plan this month?

Most of the time we are the audience we seek to provide content for. What kind of content do you buy or engage with? And if you do buy big complicated stuff are you likely to buy some random dudes homebrew campaign setting adventure module that has a cast of thousands of unheard of characters or are you more likely to buy an established official module like Curse of Strahd or the remake of Castle Caldwell? You don't usually take risks on random modules I am sure. And if you are that kind of person, check out my Mystic Times range. This is true of not just our gaming content but most media. You will find that movies like James Bond and The Avengers always do way better than just random movies with similar plots and characters made by smaller studios. We know what to expect and our understanding of the tropes in play grants us the ability to see more complicated things scattered throughout.

Making easy to access content solves a problem the audience has. Modular, easy to insert content allows them to inject their own lore into the game whilst giving players something to do.

Even when I do buy someone else's module I usually strip it down to its bare parts, a map, a quest, and some NPCs so that I can fit it into my own storylines. The number of times I have used the maps from Dungeon Delve 4e or that one map of the dwarven fortress from Thunderspire Labyrinth is uncountable.

I have also found this with Cthulhu modules on the Miskatonic Repository. The best ones pick a single, simple theme and explore it in depth, as opposed to lightly touching on hundreds of random encounters. Keeping content simple and accessible is all a part of keeping that barrier to entry as low as possible.

If you want to convert imagination into currency you need to make products people want to buy. This is a lesson that took me a long time to work out.

Activity - Taking Stock

Time for your first activity. You want to make money, you gotta work. As you continue to read this book I want to give you some active things you can do. Here is the first one. Over the next couple of days I want you to reflect and make a list of what YOU buy as a customer. Specifically I want you to follow these steps

Day 1 and 2 - Make a list, without looking at your collection, of the books and resources you use most as a game master and player. What are the things you keep coming back to—be very specific. I don't just want "the DMG," I want the list to have the exact thing you use from that resource, like "magic item rules" or "traps and hazards." Whatever it is. We all have books we get off the shelf or access on our google drive frequently. I want to see which ones really stick with you. Make sure you do this from memory. I want to know the ones you THINK are your go to resources without cheating.

Day 3 - Now that you have a list from your memory, you can take a look at your collection and see if there are any gems that you forgot from your memory. I am certain you will have books which you forgot you get out and check all the time. Add these to your list but keep them seperate from the first list.

Day 4 - If you, like me, are an old hand and veteran at this GMing thing, make another list of things you used to be obsessed with but don't look at now. For me, I used to adore the starship deckplans in the old d20 Star Wars book. I don't look at them anymore as I often make my own with computers now, but back in the day that was my lifeblood. Think about old editions, are there any books or resources from previous editions that you no longer use but could see being useful today? Or maybe you are crossing the streams, does Cthulhu need a starship deckplan book? Make a list of resources you don't use anymore but could be useful, either to new Game Masters or in a new context.

Day 5 - Now you have a list of stuff you should be making, head over to DrivethruRPG and see if those books already exist. Do some market research. If they do, how well are they selling? Could you make something better or different to what is available? How are you going to make sure your products stand out? Knowing not only what you use, but also what already exists, is going to give you a guide to not making the same mistakes.

Scope and Perfection - King vs Martin

Who would you rather be? The publisher of 200 products, each one making you a few bucks a month, or the publisher of 5 products with everyone upset at you because you haven't released the next one yet? This is the "Stephen King vs. George R. R. Martin" problem. Martin is somewhat of a perfectionist who takes great care in crafting every tiny nuance of his plot. Whilst many fans of his work do enjoy the finer details of his character building and plot structure, I have the same feelings about the series of movies Firestarter and Carrie based on the books by Stephen King. King pumps out books like crazy, and the fans of his work find just as much depth in the much shorter and easily digestible works as any scholar could in Game of Thrones.

Once you find your tribe, they will want to purchase your products for more content. It is always better to have a mediocre product that is finished than a perfect product that is still in your head.

Joyce Carol Oates often gives the advice "practice finishing" in her speeches. Finishing is something that does take some getting used to. Having a finished project also has a psychological benefit. The dopamine hit that comes from looking back at even just a single completed "thing" can not be overstated. And over time as you collect these finished projects you start to build a legacy and that is always encouraging.

No one will care about the perfection of your craft as much as you will. What people want is to enjoy your imagination and share those experiences with you. Please take it from me that most people will skim the deeper stuff anyway. Trust me, when I am not pretending to be a publisher my real job is as an English Teacher in high school and the amount of work I have to do to get students to appreciate a fairly surface level nuance year in and year out proves that few people will see your true genius let alone appreciate it.

The business model I advocate these days is one of scope rather than perfection. More products means more passive income. That is not to say make tonnes of garbage, pumping and dumping content. Still make good stuff. But be willing to release it in short bursts rather than lengthy tomes. This has the added advantage of allowing you to present a clear, focussed message which will tighten up your ability to finish a project.

Chapter 2 - Building a Community

In 2003 I downloaded a pirated version of a program called "FRAPS" and started recording myself playing video games. I really enjoyed doing that and was finding a way to put them online on a website so that I could show people. This was before YouTube was a thing and Flash Animation was the big thing. My friends in my high school made fun of me for doing that saying, "Pfft, who would want to watch someone else play video games!" And taking that to heart I stopped doing something I enjoyed. Fast forward to today and a few months ago someone at Twitch.tv leaked a list of how much income streamers are making and it's actually in the millions for the top tier. Thousands of video gamer YouTube channels exist and are getting paid sponsorships. And here is little old me, wishing I had ignored the idiots I went to high school with.

I tell you that story because whatever cool thing you enjoy doing, I guarantee you someone else enjoys the fact that you do it. Time and time again we see that they are often willing to pay money to help you keep doing it. The advantage we have today is that there are a wide variety of ways to find those communities and get our voices heard. Between websites, forums, social media, reddit, patreon, kickstarter, word press, and an endless other set of distribution networks, it has never been more abundantly clear that finding your tribe is just a matter of consistency.

I want to start with a word of warning though. People can detect posers. If you are trying to infiltrate a group to cash in, you will be outed by them. I am part of many social media groups for creators and on a daily basis I will witness some "outsider" join a group day one and post saying they are long time members, drop a product link and then never be heard from again. This kind of post always ends up ridiculed and left unsolicited.

A lot of this chapter is going to be talking about social media engagement, however all of the same rules apply to any form of communication. Whether it's meeting your friendly local gaming shop players, running events at conventions each year, or communicating with your readers in your publications, the principles are always the same.

What is far more effective in every circumstance is consistent, authentic engagement. Let's talk about what that is.

Consistent and Authentic Engagement

Engagement is a two way street. If you want more people to interact with your stuff, then you have to authentically engage with theirs. I often see artists and writers complaining that "the algorithm" is preventing their stuff from getting out there. My fellow admins at The Stash will tell you I am also known to do this kind of whinging from time to time. The truth is that the algorithm often does show your content, but no content is that great that we go out of our way to react. What is true is that community members support the others in the community that they see supporting them. It is a give and take relationship. If you only want to take you will get nothing back.

If you want success you need to help build your community. Notice I am not saying "if you want to make money you need to post everyday." I am very deliberately phrasing this in a way that removes the money from the equation. A lot of "how to make money" guides talk about this idea that consistent community engagement is what drives success, but I want to go a step further and tell you that from experience I know you can post every day and have no one give two shits about your work. The mentality of exploiting your community to make money is inauthentic and shallow. It's also a bad approach that will only lead you to failure. If you want to succeed you need to help build and grow the social links you want to use to support yourself.

Looking at this aspect of the job from the perspective that we are members of a digital village helping each other out will change the way you approach marketing and even the services you are providing your community. People work hard for their money. Most folks are living paycheck to paycheck. Few of us could survive an emergency that made us lose our income for three months or more. So if you want those people's livelihood, you better be providing a service to them that is valuable. Part of that service is about lifting up their posts and their endeavours. Liking, commenting and sharing the things they enjoy putting out into the community. Helping them get out of the algorithm black hole. You will find the more generous you are with your time towards them, the more relationships you will build online, and the stronger your community is when you ask for their support.

This is about building authentic relationships, real connections and a sense of connectedness that is more than superficial. Conveniently, doing such a thing on a consistent basis is also rewarded by every algorithm social media has. All content platforms reward consistent engagement. The more you engage with someone the more you both see each other's content.

Activity - Authentic Engagement
Okay, so at some future date you are going to have a product. That's great. Now how do people magically hear about it? Let us say you want to post it to facebook groups, reddit, twitter etc. Guess what, if you just stroll in there and spruik your wares, you are going to get next to zero response. So how do we fix this? Right now, before you have any products, you need to start engaging your community. Here's our activity:

Pick a day and if you are going to do this weekly, fortnightly, monthly, etc. That day is going to be your "engagement day." This is the day that you are going to just dedicate 30 minutes to an hour and a half just going online and spreading the love. Your first engagement day is likely to be just making a list of places you are going to visit each engagement day. Save the links in a document somewhere so you can go on every time and get there straight away.

The goal of an engagement day is to earn a bit of street cred and karma. By authentically going on reddit or facebook or whatever and helping others find success you can really develop that mutual community we have been talking about. Review other people's products. Comment on other peoples threads in a positive way. You want to help others by supporting their work. This will slowly make you a familiar face for others, so when you finally post your own stuff you won't look like a poser. Guess what, you won't look like a poser because you authentically will have built relationships and community. Surprise, I tricked you into being a nice person, but in the long run I am sure you will thank me.

Avoiding Toxicity

If you view your engagement as "building a community" rather than "exploiting a market" you will by default avoid many of the terrible things that happen online. This can be a lot harder than it sounds. It is very easy and in vogue to be negative. Shitting on things makes us feel socially powerful in the short term and those kinds of content headlines often get good interaction and analytics as well. The problem is that in being negative like that you will create a community that thrives on deconstruction and destruction. Is that who you want reviewing your products, chatting in your discord or patreon feeds and commenting on your own hard work?

By role modelling positivity you will stand out from the crowd and set the tone for how we communicate in our tribe. As a content maker (of any kind) you are the leader of discourse. The way you approach things will influence how people speak back to you. The best way to avoid having a toxic fanbase is to not be toxic yourself. Some good examples I have seen from my own content engagement would be Goobertown Hobbies, Midwinter Minis, the folks over at Pulp Alley, and Bridgett Jeffries of the Miskatonic University Podcast.

Loyalty Comes from Consistency

If you want loyal customers and fans then you unfortunately have to be consistent in your product. Producing regular content on a consistent basis is one of the toughest things we have to do. Coming up with new ideas every week (or in some cases, every day) can feel like a chore and is not for the faint hearted. This is especially true if you want to see people actually engage with your content.

This often leads to creators taking one of two paths. Either they work hard to pump and dump content that is substandard or they start varying the focus of their content until they lose their identity. Both lead to losing that loyalty you have worked hard to cultivate. It is important to keep focus on why you are making the things you are making. Ultimately you want to provide a useful service to your community, so try not to stray from that goal. The rewards of posting consistent content is that your portfolio as a whole comes across as more cohesive and professional. This attracts new members to your tribe. This is especially important when starting out.

My best advice for this would be to actually take it into consideration when you are first planning how you want to be building your community. In the beginning we start off eagerly wanting to post things once every day and making every post a lengthy piece of work. This will only lead to burn out. If you establish a cadence that is realistic early on then it becomes easier to manage over time. There is nothing wrong with posting your own content only once or twice a week so long as it happens the same time each week. If people know "THAC0 Thursday" is when you will post a video about a 2nd ed D&D resource, then they will be there on Thursday waiting.

Also consider making easy-to-make content, regularly. You can tell when I am busy in my real life because at The Stash my posts will be shops, quests or other table like content that requires less brain power. Surprisingly these small useful resources generally do far better than the stuff I pour my heart and soul into. I am thankful to have these easy resources and my top tip to the other admins who are having a hard time posting regularly is to find something like this that they can knock out in 10 minutes on a bathroom break if they are creatively blocked or busy. If you establish these kinds of "low effort - high output" content in your rotation then you can rely on them when you're having a bad time.

Gathering the Tribe

The time will come where you will realise that seemingly overnight you have gone from a few hundred followers to suddenly having tens of thousands of people subscribed to your content. It will reach a critical mass where it grows without you having to do anything but maintain those bridges and create consistently. As an example, when I first started writing this book The Stash had 14,000 followers and now we are up to 17,000. In your mind you may feel the sudden creative surge and get a product ready for release expecting them all to buy your work and support you financially. In your mind you do the maths; "if every one of them just gave me $1 that would be 3 months pay." This is quickly juxtaposed by the feeling after you release your product and post where they can find it where your heart breaks because you make only a few dozen sales.

Not everyone who follows you is going to support every product you release. Gathering the tribe is one of the hardest things you can do, especially if your plan is to take rather than give. Let's talk about why that is.

For every post you make, it will likely only be seen by about 10% of the followers you have. And of that pool of people only 1% are going to interact with it. If the call to action is making a financial purchase that then brings that number down depending on the product and its usefulness.

This is why building a marketing campaign is so important. You want to use your consistent and authentic engagement to drive interest in what you plan to release. Look at how big studios do it. They release some cool artworks, and some teaser posts, and for months beforehand they are talking with people about what to expect, and they go on as guests on podcasts and get reviewers to do some hype work and then ask you to sign up for a pre-order and then launch their kickstarter or release their product or what have you. The amount of time invested in building interest in the product is done long before its ready. Building a buzz is a long and difficult process and not everyone can master it.

This is where learning about copywriting is powerful. Copywriting is the art of writing product descriptions in a way that excites and engages an audience. The principles of this can be applied to all your marketing campaigns, not just the product's release itself. Gathering your tribe should be a joyous occasion. And if you lay the groundwork with authentic engagement along the way then the people who follow you will feel like they have been on this product development journey with you and therefore feel more invested in what you are making.

One final word about gathering your tribe. It is very reminiscent of "the boy who cried wolf." If you act like everything you do is a huge release, then people will stop listening when you try to get them excited. If you only get excited when there is actually something productive happening then people will likely join you. Remember, it's not about what your content does for you, but what it does for your audience. If your release is a self indulgent campaign guide that publishes your homebrew content that no one is interested in, then expect no one to be interested in it except you. If your release is a useful, generic collection of content they can copy-pasta into their next session then that is very useful and you will get more traction.

Only gather the tribe when what you have to share will actually help them.

The Rest of the Book

From here on out the following chapters are about individual approaches one can take to try and capitalise on the hobby we all love. Feel free to skip over them as you need to, but I would recommend skimming them at some point. You never know when an idea or inspiration might strike for something that even I haven't tried. Also please read the final chapter of the book where I will include some other helpful hints that relate to many approaches.

Chapter 3 - Adventures in Writing

Okay, so we have talked about the plan and how to build a receptive audience, but what exactly should we be creating. Well the truth is the rest of this book will look at a wide variety of ways to cash in on game mastering. I want to preface what happens next with the idea that whatever gets you paid is what you should do. Assuming you have fun doing it of course. We are going to take a look at some very weird and out of the box stuff as we go on, but let's start with the most obvious first.

Writing Adventures

The most clear cut path to making money as a gamemaster is to just sell your prep work. Writing adventures lets you do all the fun logistical behind the scenes stuff and then get it recorded for posterity. If you are really lucky you might even sell a few along the way. There is a long history of game masters making whole companies out of selling adventures. Heck, the arguably most famous D&D setting, Forgotten Realms, spawned out of one guy's home games. As did Warcraft, the world's leading fantasy computer franchise.

Writing adventures in an official way is fun and rewarding. It lets you give structure to what formerly would have been loose notes. Creating a visually interesting way to present your adventure is also heartwarming. Every time I see an adventure I have written up printed I get a giddy burst of excitement. "I made that!" I say to myself.

But writing for your home game and writing for publication are two very separate entities. For starters there are legal ramifications and many complicated documents that you have to be aware of. You should also be aware of copyright laws and how infringing on them can impact you. There is nothing worse than seeing someone work very hard on developing their first product only to see them release it, and then see it get removed from the store less than a week later, because they didn't legally have the rights to use certain art or content.

For instance, did you know that if you are planning to write Dungeons and Dragons content there are monsters in the Monster Manual that are off limits. And they aren't all ones that you would think are obvious—be aware of what your legal responsibilities are before you start all the hard work.

There are many courses and tutorials for how to write your adventures. Personally I can highly recommend the Story Telling Collective "write your first adventure" modules. Not only will they walk you through the process, but they have built great avenues for creators to share resources. Also if you finish on time your release is included in the bundle, giving you a massive boost to sales that you won't see anywhere else.

Selling Adventures

Selling the adventure is the harder part of writing the adventures for money. There are many methods by which you can distribute your work. Self publishing has never been easier than today. Making use of the existing market places will give you an active audience who are looking to buy exactly what you are after. DriveThruRPG.com is the go to place to distribute self published adventures. Sales made through them do often have a percentage of the cost taken but that is a small price to pay for access to their marketing.

If you have a following you can also sell through your own avenues. Getting a woocommerce/zendesk website up and running takes a few days' work or can be paid and done with relative ease. The problem here then becomes a question of traffic. How do you drive traffic to your website and convince them to buy? If you did have that power, why wouldn't you drive them to drivethrurpg where your audience base is going to be larger anyway.

Selling in person can also be rewarding. Taking your product to local game shops and asking them to put it on the shelf will get met with mixed results. I generally only try this with gaming shops I attend personally. You can also sell at conventions if you can afford a booth and travel times. Markets and craft fairs are also good social spots and if you attend with some regularity they can also make for great social media fodder. Just be aware that selling in person may require liability insurance. Also depending on the license you designed your content with you may be in breach of their rules.

Activity - Roll for Legalese
Read the entire SRD (System Reference Document) for 5e Dungeons and Dragons. Even if you plan on selling something for another game, you should be familiar with the legal requirements of the biggest game producer in the world. If you cannot wrap your head around this document, you may consider reaching out to someone who already publishes content for advice.

Understand what is and isn't allowed. Which creatures can't be included in your book? Which parts of character creation can you publish? What are the rules for showing that your product is suitable for 5e Dungeons and Dragons? There are so many areas that you need to fully understand to publish and it is your job to understand these things.

Guilds, Repositories, and Soloing the Battle

The biggest hurdle to selling your adventures is finding an active audience who are willing to buy it. This is where community content programs come in. The Dungeon Masters Guild, the Miskatonic Repository and the Storytellers Vault are great examples of community content programs where you can sell your wares. Personally I find many of the sales I make come from these methods of distribution. It is a production line with a built in audience that are often more than willing to try out new writers.

There is a downside to publishing with these methods however, and that is that your control of your product may be limited by their terms of sale. A great example of this is that you may ONLY sell your product through DriveThruRPG if you publish with these services. This means you can't list these items on your own website or technically sell them printed at a convention. Printing is another example of legalese rules, you cannot get them printed in physical copies unless you meet certain requirements. Personally I like to have my books on the shelf to look at.

If you are going to go solo, be aware that you are then legally responsible for the distribution of your content. This brings with it levels of liability and compliance that must be adhered to. It's also more difficult to manage and there is a learning curve to developing your product in compliance with printing standards etc. that will have to be taken into consideration. Personally I prefer to have control over my product, but that comes at a big hit to sales and a need to be entirely engaged with the legal side of things.

At the end of the day only you can choose what method of production is best for you. For beginners I would highly recommend doing a course with the Storytelling Collective and publishing with a guild/repository to get the hang of it and also make some extra money.

Activity - Read the Contract
Now that you are familiar with the SRD for publishing your own content for Dungeons and Dragons, take a look at the rules of the Dungeon Masters' Guild. What are the advantages? What are the disadvantages? What are you still not allowed to do? What things can you do under the SRD that you can not do under the Guild?

Activity - Branching Out
If you are playing other games regularly, check to see if they have community partnership programs. Some companies have their own versions of the Guild, such as The Miskatonic Repository for Cthulhu games, or Storytellers Vault for Vampire the Masquerade. Like with the SRD, you need to read the legalese and learn the rules for writing content.

Your Biggest Fan

You are your own biggest fan when it comes to campaigns and

homebrew. No one else really cares unless you have built a follower base that is already invested. You can accomplish this by writing and selling fiction successfully, or getting a loyal fan base from streaming/podcasting. In general however, no one is interested in "your world". Keep this in mind when you are constructing your adventures for sale. You are far more likely to make money from an interesting generic adventure than one that is set in a bizzare homebrew world that confuses and disinterests people.

Do not feel disheartened though. Over time, with authentic consistent engagement you can build that following. Look at R.A. Salvatore, author of arguably the most famous D&D character, Drizzt Do'Urden. Even he had to write several novels for a popular setting before he could gain enough traction to get his Demonwars setting into print. Even the greats have to make this sacrifice, working with what is already popular before they can carve their own way in the world. And with social media and streaming/podcasting building that following has never been easier to do. You will get there one day, but my advice for now is to produce marketable stuff that people want to buy.

Activity - Action Plan

If you are planning to take this route, make yourself an action plan for how you plan to learn the things you do not yet know about publishing. Make sure to include what legalities you need to learn, what distribution methods you want to explore, how do you obtain an ISBN for your product, how will you advertise your product, will you have physical stock or just digital, and other questions you might need to be familiar with. Take your time to learn each of these things and be clear about your answers.

Chapter 4 - Running Games

The next way to get paid, and personally one of my favourite ways, is to actually get paid to run games. Now, it's not as easy as it sounds as most people don't want to pay you for this service as they often get it for free. Additionally if you are getting paid then the quality of your service had better be outstanding. Every player has to feel involved and respected. Managing bad players becomes imperative. In addition, the content of your game had better be very entertaining and appropriate for all players giving you money.

Personally I enjoy running games and see it as another way to build community. You get to talk to players about their experiences, playtest your adventures, and often this leads to a marketing opportunity as you can spruik your wares during the process. Running games also often provides a key service beyond just running the game; often you are running for a community group such as a school holiday event, or charity; or perhaps for a promotional event aimed at converting to sales, such as a convention or in a shop. Be aware that running games comes with a whole range of concerns and issues that you will need to be prepared for.

Setting Expectations and Using Safety Tools

[Content Warning: Birth story]
The most important part of getting paid to run a game is to be aware of what the expectations are. This is true of both your employer and your clients. Depending on who you are working for, you may be expected to cover certain content or push certain upsells. Other employers might expect you to have a more proactive approach in handling players, this is particularly true if you are running for young people. At any rate all games you are paid to run will see you placed in the position of "representative" of whatever larger organisation you are being paid by. You must be able to live up to their expectations.

The first and most obvious of these is always going to be that your table is a safe and appropriate place for your clients. I do not care what you personally think about certain suggested practices, at the end of the day your job as a game master in a paid game is to ensure that every single member of that table has a good time. This will mean that you will need to have strategies ready for making it clear how you will deal with issues like problem players or concerning content. An excellent way to do this is to begin with a discussion that clearly states the group's expectations.

This does not have to be super formal. But it does need to be agreed upon by all players at the table. Every person has a hand in making sure the gaming table is a safe and fun place to be. This is also good practice for your home games too.

Personally I start this conversation with a discussion of "the golden rule" and "Wheaton's Law." The golden rule, as has been written in many a dungeon master guide for decades is "Everyone should be having fun" and this rule trumps all other rules. If the book says one thing and that is going to cause problems, then fun should trump unfair restrictions etc. Sometimes it is important to remember that restrictions are often there to ensure that fun is had and some degree of balance exists within the game. "Wheaton's Law," named after Wil Wheaton is officially "Don't be a dick," though depending on your clients you may have to rephrase this. The premise is simple, don't do things to actively cause grief for others. Generally speaking, between these two rules you should cover most things that other rules might encompass. Things like "Speaking over others," "Respecting others," and "Not doing [x]" will be covered by this. I usually ask if there are any other rules that people want put in place and we talk about this as a group. It is important not to let this discussion get too carried away as "time is money, friends." Giving players the opportunity to add anything specific is always a hero GM move.

The second thing I generally like to discuss is how to handle content that is controversial. You, as a game master, can not read minds. You need to have a system for dealing with triggers and concerning events. Before you start reacting and using the word "snowflake" in response to me, let me tell you a story. Generally I do not care about most things and am not touchy feely. I have a dark sense of humour and am generally dead inside. On the day that my son was born, there was a moment during that process where we almost lost him. That is a long and complicated tale, but needless to say everything turned out alright and I have moved on with my life. Or so I thought. I was in a game and the players were talking about the compression socks that they put on you in hospital. Random right? But for some reason I have a super strong sense memory of the image of those socks being put on my wife and the moment we almost lost my son. They were going to send her into an emergency caesarean and as all the chaos was happening this one nurse was trying to put the socks on my wife and asked me to help. A tiny detail in a huge story. As a result of it being brought up in a game, I started to get a little teary and emotional as all the stress and fear of that one moment came flooding back. It wasn't a big deal. I just needed 30 seconds to recompose myself. If someone had asked me "Do you need a trigger warning for socks?" I would have laughed at them. Chances are talking about socks isn't likely to trigger that emotional response again and I could never have predicted that in that moment I would react the way I did.

The fact of the matter is that you do not know what could possibly be a trigger for everyone of your closest friends. Heck, you might not even know what might trigger you to feel some kind of sense memory. So as such it is important to have a system in place to deal with that. There are many great examples of systems in place and I have tried many of them. A simple google search for "Safety Tools," "X cards," and "Lines and Veils" are all great places to start. The Miskatonic University Podcast has a great episode on Safety Tools and I encourage everyone to go and listen to that.

After many years I personally have come up with a simple system that I like to use these days called "the traffic lights." If in person, I will give each player 3 poker chips/coloured cards, one green, one yellow, and one red. We all know how traffic lights work so it's pretty easy to explain. Whichever one is on the top, that's what is going on. If everyone is green, happy days. If a player hears something that concerns them then they might switch to a yellow card which means "slow down", or a red card which means "stop." If we see red, we stop for a break and ask them what needs to be changed. They do not have to go into detail or retraumatise themselves, but you do need to know what not to do. That is the only information you need, do not ask questions. If we see yellow they might suggest a different course of action, or they might be okay to just continue on, being wary of their emotions.

This system is superior to some of the other systems because it doesn't require players to "out" themselves about what their trauma is. Also it gives them the option to slow down rather than bring things to a complete stop. I have had many games where a player will flash a yellow card, and then once we move into the next scene they go back to green. It can be a way of just pre-warning the GM that they are worried where the game is headed. It also doesn't require a person to pre-meditate on what causes them grief. Like I said, I didn't know I was going to get freaked out by a sock. This system works in that instance.

Whatever system you decide to use is up to you, but you should make it clear to your players that this is the way you plan to handle it. Much like the above "rules" discussion it takes all of 10 seconds to explain a system and what to do. Most gamers will get it straight away. I am yet to have a player in a professional game get offended by me suggesting a system.

How are problem players going to be dealt with? This is also a brief but important discussion. Personally I like to have a 3 strike rule, you get one "warning," and one "oopsy," but on the 3rd strike you are removed from the game. If you are running publicly you will need to have this ready. Of all the tips I have learnt about running public games, this is the number one thing that comes up. There will always be a player who gets on other peoples nerves. On the one hand, that player does have a right to be there too, so it can't just be social bullying because that person is a bit awkward. In fact that kind of ostracising behaviour is one that I will give a strike to everyone else for. But if that player's actions become harmful to the group dynamic then it is important that it be dealt with. This can be done privately in a "short break to go over your notes" or publicly at the table depending on how you believe that sort of a thing will go down. Reading a table and a trouble maker is a complicated task. If you side with the aforementioned Wheaton's Law and the concept you are trying to provide a safe space for people to have fun, then I generally find most problem behaviour settles itself down. Again there are a million resources for dealing with this that can be found online. As with all the conversations, it shouldn't take forever to establish "the rules". Just a brief conversation to set expectations.

Some other fun discussions might be about social media, phone use, etc. I think that phones and photographs are often frowned upon at the table, but what can be really invigorating is to get people taking photos of key moments in the game or posting quotes to twitter and sharing a group hashtag. Not everyone will want to be a part of that, but if you can get that going it can be good for business, especially in a shop or convention. Generally I like to get groups to take a group shot at the start, get it out of the way, and then put the phones away so we don't get distracted. That being said, every group is different. Sometimes this kind of a conversation might be happening because of a store/convention policy. Often groups with young people are prohibited from taking the photos because of legal reasons. Some people might just not want randoms taking their photo and that is also an acceptable reason to have a no photo policy. Please be conscious of these sorts of policies.

Finally you need to make it clear what kind of game you are running. Is this a "PG13" game or a more mature game? Will there be lots of political negotiations or is it a dungeon crawl? This helps to give everyone a clear guide as to the vibe to go for and gets everyone on the same page. Whilst this isn't strictly necessary, it doesn't hurt things to spend under a minute managing what people think.

Once expectations are managed it is time to get on with the show. As mentioned, maybe 5 minutes total should be spent on this. It isn't a big impact on the setting up of the game, but you will be thankful you did it when the inevitable issue arises.

Activity - Building a Safety Toolbox
Do some research on safety tools, their importance, and various different ways of implementing them. You might also want to spend some time doing some research on conflict management strategies as a part of this. The more tools you as a game master have in your toolbox, the easier things will go.

Activity - Preflight Checklist
Make yourself a brief preflight checklist for any future paid games you might run.

Include what rules you would like to follow, any safety tools you plan to use, your problem player policy, and anti-distraction tactics. Once you have this checklist established, the whole process will become fairly smooth. Take some time to rehearse the way you might put this to players and be conscious of the time you are taking to go through the list and explain. Also consider how you will discuss any "reactions" to your checklist. What are you going to do if the problem player begins trying to hijack your "snowflake checklist" as you explain it? What will you do if there is a rules dispute? What would you do if one cluster of players want an R18+ game but another cluster want PG13? Preparing mentally for this is a good practice.

Running for Shops

The most common approach people have to trying to get paid for running is to approach their local gaming shop. This is also the least likely option on the list to get paid with - a paradox, to be sure. Running games for shops, like running games for any business, requires you to come at things from the shop's perspective. Often you will be making use of a public space in the shop that could be used for games that generate more income than your game will. You will be adding risk to their public liability insurance and also risk to their public image. If you are volunteering to run for a shop and run a bad game, then "la dee da it was just a bad game. Sorry folks," but if you are getting paid to run for a shop and a player isn't happy with the game now you are an employee/subcontractor who is causing damage to the shop's reputation. It is a risk for them to accept your request, and in most cases they are going to have other people offering to do what you are doing for free anyway.

The Good Old Fashioned Gaming Shop

Your best bet to get a paying gig at a Friendly Local Gaming Store (FLGS) is to approach them with a proposal for a promotional event of some kind. Perhaps you can offer to showcase a new game that has come out, or perhaps you are offering a seasonal game that will drive sales of another product. As an example, Let us say that your FLGS are big Arjade's Productions fans and the latest "Call of Glory" adventure module has just been released. You know that they want to sell as many copies as they can so perhaps you offer to run 5 weeks of promotions for them where you will run the dungeons in that adventure book each week to showcase the product and push sales. You can also make it a requirement that every player bring in a miniature that they have purchased from this shop, and that they have their own dice set. In addition to this you will purchase your own copy of "Call of Glory" from them, adding to their sales numbers. You might even suggest that the miniatures used to play this could be entered into a painting competition judged by the store, driving sales of paints and brushes as well. Now chances are that they still won't be all that impressed, but hey, you gave it your best shot.

Whatever way you approach a FLGS to ask to be paid to run a game, keep in mind that they are more likely to go with someone who has clearly organised something special, thought it all through, and made a compelling case than they are to go with someone who is planning to just wing it. Often these kinds of promotional ideas will be a part of the shop's strategy anyway and staff will be taking the role of Game Master.

Babysitting Duty

Another approach that I often find works is to offer your services during School Holidays times. This is good for me as I am a teacher when I am LARPing as a functional adult and I have those days off anyway. Often FLGS become dumping grounds for bratty nerds during school holiday times. As a former FLGS employee I can tell you that I would happily pay for someone else to be in charge of the random kids that would turn up only during holidays just to lurk and be a pain in everyone's side. This obviously comes with its own issues. I can tell you first hand that running games for kids/teens are some of the most challenging "group management" concerns I have ever faced, and that includes being a teacher. Also the content of your games has to be on par with what would be expected during such a session. Depending on where you live it wouldn't hurt to have a current "Working With Children Check" or equivalent as well. And let's not even get started talking about the parents. Haha. Okay so maybe this wasn't the best idea. But in all seriousness, be aware that this is an option. If you are already good with young people and don't mind running a kid friendly table this can be a profitable source of seasonal income for a GM to cash in on. If you are close enough to multiple stores or don't mind driving, you can even schedule sessions on multiple days of the week and rotate employers.

Hipster Adjacent

Another approach is to not run in a gaming store at all. You would be surprised by the number of nerd-friendly establishments there are out there. Being a geek these days is in vogue, and how many bougie cafes and restaurants have "board game corners" or "book nooks" and the like. If you were really wanting to be entrepreneurial and wanted to try your luck you could always put together a proposal for somewhere that was nerd-adjacent. For cafes and the like your selling point is that whilst your players are there they are going to be buying beverages and food.

The sales come to the cafe in the form of consumables. This is going to have a low profit margin for them however. You will be taking one or two tables which usually would rotate throughout the day and have a high turnover of consumables and be replacing it with six to ten people who are going to purchase several drinks and maybe a single meal. It isn't the best deal for them. This can be overcome with a cover charge for the game (ie entry fee) that may be split between the GM and the employer. Another way to approach such a proposal is to pitch it to them as a promotional opportunity. Suggest that the group can be photographed having a fun time and that those photos can be used for their social media pages and promotional materials. This of course means that the player base will have to agree to that when signing up for the game. Depending on the location this may be a great selling point for them.

Do keep in mind that if you are going to try running for a non-gaming shop, they may not be familiar with what is involved. Roleplaying gets a little loud and rowdy sometimes. Allowing the employer to make an informed decision is important in this instance. It would be very bad if you were trying to pitch such an event and the employer was expecting it to be a quiet little get together rather than the dragonslaying, dungeoneering brawlfest that it can become. Likewise you need to establish the space requirements and expectations with the employer as well. If they are expecting you to sit eight people in a tiny cubicle there might be an issue with that. These kinds of events might also be good for "after hours exclusive" events. Some cafes and restaurants hold trivia nights and things of that nature after hours. This could be a great example of something that could get them a little extra business after hours in the same vein.

Be a Considerate Symbiote

Wherever you end up running, if you are running for a shop there are many things to consider. Does the shop have rules that are going to be important to consider. Does your event have a strict time frame (ie does the shop close dead on 7pm, have a midnight closing restriction from the local council, or something else) and how will you structure the game around that. How much is the shop expecting you to push their products? Are you comfortable with that? Is this a special event or an ongoing arrangement? It is no good getting paid $100 for what you think is 6 sessions if they decide that you are going to do it for the whole year for that price. Can you make it to the sessions you are signing up to? In the foreword to this book I discussed my first time getting paid for running games. That gig was located 2 and a half hours' drive from my work/home. Every week for 6 weeks I had to drive through peak hour/post work traffic to be able to get there on time, and then I would run for three hours and then drive home. It became a real struggle and although they offered me the opportunity to be paid well to do that every single week for the rest of the year I could not commit to that peak-hour commute. You might also have to consider what happens if you or someone else gets sick. As we have seen in the past few years, Covid has locked down most of these kinds of events in shops. If you have been paid to run 6 sessions and the shop gets locked down after session 3, what happens with the money? Do you have to give a refund? These are just a few of the potential hurdles you are going to have to face. Welcome to the world of business, friend.

Running paid games for shops can be some of the most fun times that you can get paid for as a game master. If you can find a way to get paid for such a thing, make sure that you truly appreciate that opportunity. Support your local gaming shops because without them the local gaming community fizzles. You might also find that you can use such games as a marketing opportunity for your other hustles. Perhaps you don't get paid to run the game, but they do allow you to advertise your "GM for hire" business there. Or perhaps they even might stock your adventure modules and sell them on a commission basis for you. Try not to overextend the friendship however.

Activity - Location Audit

Make a list of the locations around you that could be potential hosts for your pitch to run paid games. Consider what you are bringing to the table that they can't already get. Try to put yourself in the shoes of the business owner and assume they know nothing about you or what you want to do. What kinds of questions are they going to ask and how can you answer them? Be sure to never promise anything you can't back up. You might not have a FLGS but where else can you offer to run? What kind of payment would you be expecting? What are some hazards you can identify with running at that location and how do you plan to mitigate them? What will you do when a non-player comes to "watch" (aka lurk) and makes everyone else feel self-conscious? What will you do when a paying customer complains that the game is too loud, or too adult to want their children to overhear?

Activity - Practice Pitch
Imagine you have found a gaming store "Fake Games" that is open to a paid GMing opportunity. How can you make the sessions you plan to run a successful business promotion for them? How will you get money in the register each session? How long will your promotion run for? How will you stand out when other GMs will run games for free? What is the benefit to the business? What concerns will the business have? How do you have solutions for that concern? How will you make the players who sign up feel like they are special and contributing? How will you push products onto the players in a way that is successful? How will you deal with player issues or moments when you are representing the business? Put all these into a pitch document and then show that document to some friends and ask them to pretend they own the fictional business "Fake Games", look over the pitch and ask them to ask you hard questions about what you have put together. This can be a really good practice for actually doing a pitch in real life. It also takes some of the fear out of criticism and feedback.

Running for Conventions

Running for conventions is very different to running home games or even for a shop. Whilst they often share many similarities to running for a shop, there are many subtle differences in a convention game that make them complex to master for. If you are lucky enough to get the opportunity to run at a convention it is a great learning experience and will greatly improve your game mastering skills. You may find that you are not paid for such an event, but have the opportunity to "promote your wares" as a result of running for them. If this is the case be sure to establish the degree to which this is allowed. You want to be invited back again to the next convention don't you?

Spot the Difference

The convention crowd are a very different bunch to the FLGS crowd. Local gaming shops have regulars who are usually pretty casual and friendly. Convention crowds can be really diverse and will have players ranging from "this is literally the first time I am playing a game" to "I brought my 17th-level min-maxed Oathbreaker Paladin named Darksmite McEdgelord, they have been in 70 convention games and by the end of this one I should reach level 18." You have to be ready for gamers who have only seen memes and never a Player's Handbook sitting across from old school grognards who played the red box when it first came out. You will also have a wide array of expectations. Do the players want hack and slash or more roleplay based adventures? It is for this reason that it is important to have set expectations in the first 5 minutes of the game.

You may also find the time limits are stricter. Some convention games cycle through a story every 2 hours, over and over again. Others will have an 8 hour long haul with the same players. Being prepared and aware of the kind of game you are running is vital. Be sure to have asked this of the organiser well in advance.

In my experience the best way to approach a convention game as a GM is to treat it as a single session special event. I usually go in with pre-made characters on a sheet that is colour coded/highlighted for new players to easily find "the red bit where the attack and damage is" and prevent the level 17 min-max characters. I usually let players fill in their own roleplay stuff like names, gender, background etc. and just have pre-generated statistics. I also have a story that is self contained. Perhaps they are on a boat or train or something, travelling and can not get off. Perhaps they are locked in a dungeon/lost in a cave and must escape. The point is to start them in a closed physical space to prevent wandering off. I also tend to focus on storylines that are asking players to interact with one another. Think of it like an escape room with specialised individuals. Each player gets a clue/key to be the hero for just a moment, sharing the spotlight equally between them all. At least that is how it should run in theory.

Different conventions might have different expectations of you as a game master. You might not be allowed to promote your wares. You might have certain rules you have to follow. Maybe the convention wants to keep things PG13 even if you have a group of mature adults who want to push that boundary. It is important to remember in a convention environment, you are a part of a bigger whole (so don't be an A-hole!). You have to abide by the organisational structures in play.

This is also true when it comes to the way you treat players. At a FLGS or in home games, you might develop a casual friendship with the players you are seeing. You probably already know some of them. In a convention you are almost always dealing with strangers. Some might have come a long way to be here. Some might have come interstate or overseas. At a convention they are also choosing to roleplay with you rather than take in all the other exciting things that are happening at the event. They have placed their bets on this being the most fun part of the experience for them. As such you have a responsibility to make sure that they have a great time, feel respected and safe, and that their effort was rewarded with the game you offer them. Each one of them are V.I.P.s (Very Important Players) and you have to make sure you keep that in mind.

Because it is often a group of disparate strangers who are meeting for a limited time, organising the party is a lot more difficult in a convention game. They may have incredibly different values and personalities and might need a little encouragement to play together nicely. You have to be prepared for such a thing. Think about ways you can bring them all together in a safe and fun way.

If you have run for conventions in the past, you might like to even try spreading your wings a little bit. Perhaps you could try offering your services to non-gaming related conventions. Comic conventions, County Fairs, School Fetes, and other events can all be potential opportunities for you to get some experience under your belt. I would not recommend this to beginners as there may be many things you are not prepared for. But once you have experience with convention games this can be an excellent way to develop new potential gaming markets and community outreach opportunities.

Activity - Research
Jump online and see if you can find some conventions that happen near you. There are some people who go from convention to convention, travelling the country and making their living from this. See if you can find a number of convention dates which you could in theory attend. This may be harder these days than it used to be, but as time goes on face to face conventions may begin to grow in number once more. Make an itinerary of conventions you could one day offer to run games at. Find out if these conventions pay GMs, and what their rules are for marketing your own products.

Activity - Research II
Taking your list, attend some convention games. Build a network, talk to the GMs of the games you are playing with. Ask them how they got involved with it. During the game, look for moments when players are being a problem. Think how you could have dealt with the problems that arise. You might not even notice some problems, such as shy players or power imbalances. Try to keep an eager eye out. After the game ask the GM about the session and what they were doing to actively deal with such social issues. Ask them about how they plan their games for conventions and what tips they have for anyone wanting to have a go.

Activity - Plan a Convention Game
Take some time to plan a game specifically for a convention. Think about everything you will need to have ready. Premade characters, a closed adventure, a checklist of safety tools. Think about how you will engage players and make challenges that are interesting. Remember, any player joining you at a convention game is doing so by giving up all the other things the convention has to offer. How can you live up to their sacrifice? What are some potential triggers in your story that might be an issue for some players? How will you warn them of such things? What's the "that was amazing" moment that your players will be talking about until the next convention? How can you make sure everyone will be safe? Write this up in a formal way and make handouts that you can use again in the future.

Running as a Special Event

From time to time we will get the opportunity to run a game as a special event. These might be holiday programs, or perhaps a charity event, or maybe you are going to run a game for someone's birthday party. My wife has often joked that she would love to run games on a cruise ship, like a D&D themed cruise with sessions each day in certain timeslots. Wouldn't that be amazing? Sometimes these opportunities do arise, but only if you are looking out for them. In the case of a special event often because it is a once off chance to play you are able to charge a cover charge/entry fee for it. Some examples that I have run in the past are an Easter themed session where a huge cursed dire rabbit was turning everyone into chocolate. I made him bright pink but with matted disgusting fur covered in chocolate. It was very memorable. I have also often done Chinese New Year based celebrations for school groups, Christmas themed games for families, and an Anzac day WW2 game for veteran soldiers. Some of these were paid opportunities, others were labours of love. All of them have made me friends that I still talk to about games today.

One example that I like to talk about is School Holiday programs because that is, I think, an untapped resource. Kids frigging love roleplaying games. Once they get to the age of about 10 they are able to understand everything they need to really get the most out of the game. Unlike adults they come up with some amazing ideas and with the right kind of "Yes and..." game master they can really break the walls down on how the game is played. The game is also very useful to them. It teaches maths, problem solving, literacy, and social skills. The list goes on. If that wasn't enough, during school holidays parents are also struggling to find things for their kids to do. In the longer batches of holidays kids go crazy by the end of it and they have done all that they can do within their own four walls. Along comes extra-curricular school holidays activities programs. When I used to work at the gaming shop I would run a game every second day. Open invitation, so whoever showed up, got to play. It was lots of fun. Obviously I was being paid as an employee for that shop and so that worked out in the long run. Since then I have approached other shops, libraries, school groups, vacation care programs and even been asked by parents who are friends if I could run a private game for their kids during the holidays and been offered money for all of these opportunities. I have young people who are now approaching twenty who still talk to me about that one game I ran for them back when they were in primary school. It sticks with them. This is an example of a great opportunity for a games as a service business to develop a whole bunch of community ties, get promotions out there, and do some good for the world all at the same time.

Finding opportunities like this, and ear-marking them on your calendar year after year, is a chance for you to put some paid opportunities on your resume. Holidays are like spokes on a wheel, as the year rotates, they come up in increments. There are many reasons for this, but this means that there are regular opportunities for you to get your name out there and find great ways to maximise your business model for running games.

More Considerations for the Symbiotic GM

If you are going to try and do this however, there are some things to consider. Firstly, if you are going to approach a community group, school organisation, local library, parents association, or any other organisation, you need to be aware that they will have a lot higher expectations of you than if you were running for a shop or convention. Engaging in the community will find you often well received, but also well scrutinised. This is exceptionally true if you are working with children. You will need to have clear risk assessments, public liability insurance, itemised invoices and quotes, paperwork to demonstrate your business model and likely a working with children check. That being said, if you are able to do this and get yourself a name for running these kinds of once off, special events, then you can really pull off some consistent business throughout a year and earn some big bucks for doing it.

Consider what service you will be providing and if you have the ability to theme the game itself to match the kind of organisation you are approaching. When I used to teach at a large selective school filled with nerdy kids I used to run a game for their "Celebration Day," a large multicultural festival that was always scheduled right before the final exams and graduation of the senior students. I would usually run these games based around the theme of a spring festival as that most matched the kind of celebration that was happening around the students at that time. As most of these students wouldn't actually be gamers it was very noob-friendly. I would provide colour coded character sheets with premade characters and everyone would receive a set of dice and 3d printed mini to take home and keep. My goal for these events was to try and grow the gaming community. I would often tell the gamers about the local gaming shops near them (the students came from all over the Sydney Metropolitan area) and try to encourage them to go and find local groups of their own. Years later I still run into these ex-students from time to time and it warms my heart when they tell me they are now the game master for their friends. In this instance the goals were less financial and more community focussed. But the benefit is that they have gone on to support their local gaming shops, often places that have then paid me to run events because they heard about me through these former students.

Running events is very similar to running for a convention. You have to be very prepared and also have to be ready to socially manage your (often inexperienced) players. Unlike conventions, running for a group is often very profitable but will require really selling your idea to whatever group is paying you. You can cut out the middleman and run programs organised by yourself, however that requires you sourcing clients and locations. That being said, if you are already running games as a service (see below) then chances are you will have everything set up for that. I find personally that these games can be the most rewarding and fun because they are often big overblown one-shots that everyone has a good time in.

Activity - Researching Community Groups

Make a list of local community groups you are already somewhat involved in. These could be gaming groups, school based groups, churches/temples/youth groups, charities, sports teams, parents/neighbourhood groups, outreach programs, therapeutic groups, gyms, scouts/cadets/girl guides, aged care facilities, social groups like Probus Clubs, Rotary, etc. Also add to this list anything that your family members or close friends are involved in. Maybe you don't have kids, but you have nieces and nephews. Maybe you are not retired, but your aunt is and is a member of a bowling club. Think about physical clubs too, like the RSL clubs that host events. Once you have this list, pick a handful that you think might be amenable to some kind of special event game and try to think about how you could market that. An example, the RSL (Returned Services League) might be interested in a special Anzac/Remembrance Day event that you could run themed around World War two (if done respectfully). This might be a day of roleplaying or what might work better is a demo day for table top historical wargaming where you could offer demonstrations of how to play to their members. Try to think of how you might approach that in a way that builds your business. Consider if this is an event to make money or an event to build reputation. Not every event you run is about making cash, sometimes you have to build a profile instead. If your event isn't a cash grab, how can you direct the participants towards something that will provide a return in the long run?

Activity - Tournaments/Competitions/Slow Grow
Sometimes you have to think out of the box to make something special. Perhaps for a special holiday you could run some kind of tournament or competition. Think of some opportunities you could make use of and consider how you could market them in a way that is more than just running a game. An example might be that maybe to drive business on a black friday event at your FLGS you could run a game and have a list of Bingo cards for players. Each card is different but they might have things like "Crit Fail," "Crit Success," "Missed by 1," "I seduce the [monster]," "NPC was evil all along," and various other fun events that could take place. Filling the card out might mean they win a prize. This could simply be a 10% off coupon provided by the FLGS or it might be some actual thing like a dice set or some kind of hand crafted (aka cheap to make) thing. In this instance we are making something out of nothing to drive business for that day. And should the FLGS be involved they might get repeated business after the day.

This can also come in the form of an ongoing event, such as a "slow grow" wargaming campaign, or a "Cheese Eater tournament" where players make the cheesiest possible min-max build for an RPG character of [x] level and compete in gladiatorial battle to eventually see the winner. Throwing in fun twists can often make the events a bit more challenging. For instance, one of my favourite events before I started working for a shop was our FLGS ran a league of a skirmish wargame. It was a round robin league and as you fought others you got points. One week they had a "sewers only" event where you had to fight on a map that they had made. It meant that so many of the big long range armies were at a disadvantage, where previously they would dominate. When you do stuff like this it is important to reward fun, not just prowess. This is also a way to build community as players who are knocked out can then cheer on the teams they want to win the tournament. Slow grow campaigns are fun and are often a profitable endeavour for the FLGS running them as they require people to purchase new miniatures to build out an army. This is dipping into wargaming waters and away from game mastering, but you get the idea.

Have a think about your local games community and what kind of special event you could offer to organise as a promotion for them. How could you make it a profitable affair for both yourself and the FLGS?

Activity - Invoicing, Insurance, Intermittent Injuries
If you are planning on approaching community groups you will need to have everything sorted and ready in your pitch to them. This kind of pitch is different to a business pitch because you need to be a whole package independently of whatever you are running. Consider running an event for a local community group you are a part of. Make a list of all the expenses that would be incurred by you if you did get approval to run that. Consider things like insurance costs for public liability insurance, cost per player for things like dice, miniatures, pencils, paper, etc. Consider venue hire/location requirements. Write a risk assessment on the prospective location and activities. Make a list of what you would do to mitigate those risks. Consider what your own time is worth and how much you will charge for that per player. Itemise these all in a prospective invoice that you could provide to a community group. To find out what something like this might look like, you may have to research what similar organisations provide. If you are a member of an organisation that has a treasurer you might like to talk to them about what kinds of things they want to see on an invoice for such an event. This kind of thing is going to be your business now so enjoy the headaches. Haha. Don't forget to keep track of taxation requirements and how much of that potential income is taxable.

Running as a Service

Running the game as a service is a business model all of its own and there are a wide array of approaches to that. For some it's as simple as being a game master mercenary, hiring yourself out to whoever is going to pay the bounty on an awesome session. Others are trying to use their services as a way of healing and therapy, educating, teaching social skills or as a social outlet for the underprivileged or left behind. All of these services are running in a similar way to running an event for a charity or community group, except it's a business model rather than some kind of promotional event. In this section we will take a quick look at how you might approach something like this and make it profitable. All of these examples are based around the premise you are building a consistent business of marketing yourself. That implies that there is some degree of business knowledge required. Be sure to be familiar with the requirements in your country, state, county etc for starting a business.

There has never been a more popular time to be involved with roleplaying. Even just compared to a few years ago, the level of acceptance, understanding and engagement has dramatically skyrocketed for this hobby. I remember just a few years ago trying to explain exactly what roleplaying is to people and having them completely miss the point. It was infuriating watching tv shows get it 100% wrong in their portrayal trying to make it edgy or cool. But these days that is getting less and less the case as more and more people grow familiar with it through the media they consume. With that familiarity has come a range of people who don't know how to play, but know they want to. This is a market that we can tap into.

Game Master Beware

There are many freelancers and patreon driven game masters out there. Often they sell their services via social media, streaming or podcasting adjacent business models and thanks to the dramatic uptake in online gaming in the past few years this is a model that has seen great economic gain. Be it in person or online the opportunities are out there. As with all paid gigs, ensuring all your paperwork and insurances are up to date is key. You don't want to get lumped with a 1 million dollar negligence case in court because you were paid by a mum who had their kid fall off the chair they were rocking on in their own house. In addition to those kinds of issues already discussed above, if you are going to have service as a business model then you might want to formally write down your policies regarding things and have a legal representative help you establish a proper contract which you have your clients sign. This is imperative with this model of business for two reasons. Firstly it makes it legally clear what the expectations are. Be warned that this also means you must follow your own rules. Secondly, it shows the client that what you are doing is legitimate business and not just you being their friend. Boundaries are key to freelancing.

Mode of delivery is an important choice. Whilst in person definitely has a great deal of advantages in terms of providing a rewarding and engaging experience for the clients, there are a great number of additional issues it raises. What location will the game take place? Will it be in the clients home? How can you assure your safety in a stranger's home? Will it be in your home? How will you ensure your safety in your own home? Imagine you are running from your home, have a bad session, and a disgruntled client decides that they are unhappy with you and stalk or vandalise your home. If you are running a game from a client's home, how do you ensure that rules are followed or that you aren't going to get bonked on the head and sold to orcs as a slave? If meeting in public, can you ensure that you will be allowed to continue running? In a library or restaurant you may be asked to leave if your group is too noisy. If you are hiring a space, that needs to be included in your invoice and eats into your profits.

Delivering online can be a little safer as it removes a lot of these kinds of issues. Whilst it does remove a lot of the immersion and "bonuses" you can gift to your client, it means things can run smoother. It also opens your potential clients up to a world-wide basis. This can bring timezone and organisation issues, issues with payment and cybersecurity, and all kinds of other cool things I bet you never thought of. What happens if the client's internet connection keeps dropping out? They are still in the session but they are not having a good time. Do they get a refund? They ate your hours up though, so do you go unpaid? What if it is the same every week for three weeks in a row? Still giving them that refund? All of these are issues that will need to be risk assessed and clear contractual policies created.

Getting a Gig

Regardless of which choice you make, the first big step is going to be getting clients. There are many "jobs boards" available where you can sell your services. I am sure that with social media the way it is these days, making it known that you plan to have a game mastering for profit business you will easily pick up a job or two here. You will need to find a way to set a price that is both affordable to your client and profitable for you. Again this will often be trial and error. Getting your name out there is a factor which will snowball over time. If you remain consistent and reliable as a game master and a promoter, eventually you will find yourself many people who are looking to engage your services.

At the end of the day, making this choice is something you have to do for yourself. You will find opportunities will arise the more you make yourself open to them. Eventually your problem will become one of scheduling and scalability rather than the minutia of how to run your business. No matter what you decide, you will discover new and exciting issues that you need new policies for along the way. It is all part of this wonderful side hustle.

More Than Just a Game

These days there are many "gimmicks" that roleplaying is getting manipulated into in order to fit a business model. I use that word, which isn't entirely accurate or respectful and that is for want of a better term. The concept of finding your niche is one that many social media influencers have talked about for decades now, and the same is true for Roleplaying Game Mastering as a service. For many the answer is actually to use roleplaying as a tool for achieving some other means. These business models tend to be extremely successful when done correctly. Roleplaying as therapy, as education, as socialisation are all valid business strategies. It adds another layer to the business not previously accessible when roleplaying is just for entertainment purposes. The best businesses solve a problem, and being bored is just not as high up on the list as literacy, numeracy, mental health, and social skills. Regardless of the kind of game you are going to run all of these things are going to be impacted simply through the engagement with the act of roleplaying, however making that a part of your core business model takes you from "a fun school holiday program" into a "wellbeing and educational paraprofessional program." Depending on the specifics of how you build your business and who your clientele are you might even be able to access government grants or educational funding. As with everything here be sure to check what legal requirements and certifications are needed before you just jump in the deep end with some idea.

Roleplaying as therapy is something that I am very interested in. I am a qualified psychotherapist and have experience as both a youth counsellor and a crisis therapist. The concept of roleplaying actually stems from a psychological practice by Fritz Perls called "Gestalt Therapy." One of the methods of gestalt therapy is getting the client to roleplay as the different people in their life and try to understand the problem from multiple perspectives. As such roleplay and therapy go way back to decades before Dungeons and Dragons was even created. I have seen several business models using roleplaying to address some therapeutic aspect and many of them are very successful in what they set out to achieve. An article in 2017 by Raul Gutierrez discusses the theoretical impact of roleplaying games as a therapy, but whilst he is there studying it, others are out there doing it. Wheelhouse Workshop, Initiative Roll, Critical Core and many others are all engaging in this business model of hybrid roleplaying game and play therapy. This is obviously something that I would prefer be facilitated by people with psychotherapeutic certification, psychology training or experience in play therapy, youth counselling and other mental health industry certifications. But if you, like me are in a position to get involved with something like that then you can put the hard work we do as a game master to some good in this world. I would encourage you to keep an eye out for these opportunities around you, and if you get the chance support them in whatever way you can.

As a teacher I also see the great potential of roleplaying games as an educational service. I have a friend who incorporates an aspect of MMO gamification into his junior high school classes. I myself have dabbled in the odd use of RPGs with students to get them to come up with ideas for stories, character interaction, drama improv, and just increase social skills. I was given a Maths class to cover once and I used RPGs to make a rudimentary Pokémon-based game to teach them algebra. I know firsthand the good these games can do to give a framework to education that is more than just skill and drill and I highly encourage anyone considering running games as a service to think how they could incorporate educational outcomes, social outcomes and general community involvement into their business model.

Chapter 5 - Streaming/Podcasting Games

The number one most successful and profitable platform to make money off your game mastering in this book is Streaming and Podcasting games. Leaked data from twitch shows that even mid-tier streamers were getting payouts of up to USD$20,000 a year just from the donations they made on their streams alone. There are many people who have quit their jobs and education to try and become full time streamers or podcasters and a cluster of those people are successful. If you are willing to put in the time, dedication and performance energy to consistently produce good content then you too could join these people. However, just like the millions of waitresses and frycooks out there who identify as "actors waiting to be found", every man and their dog has tried their hand at podcasting and streaming. Competing on these platforms these days is a difficult thing and for every one twitch streamer who is making 20k a year, there are hundreds of thousands who are making a big old goose-egg (nothing).

When talking specifically about just streaming and podcasting games alone, the stakes for this have raised dramatically. When I first started getting into this stuff, once a year you got to see the Acquisitions Incorporated crew do a short dungeon. There were a handful of pretender podcasts and that was about it. These days, you are competing against full blown productions like Critical Role, Maze Arcana, The Adventure Zone, or Dimension 20, filled with talented voice actors, big budgets, high quality recording gear and massive fan bases. This shows the dangers associated with quitting your day job for the pursuit of this career, but also demonstrates how potentially successful you can be. Particularly if you are going to stream something that is a smaller game with a loyal following, like Cyberpunk, Edge of the Empire, or Ponyfinder. (Please let me know if you start a Ponyfinder stream because of this book! That would be amazing.)

Performers vs Your Friends

When I first got the idea in my head to have a crack at running a liveplay podcast, I thought "How hard could it be? Just record my play group, right?" And then I suddenly noticed all the little things my friends did to bug the crap out of me that would just simply not cut it on a recorded podcast. One friend who is just mopey and quiet. I had another friend who made this really awesome character, but the premise was that they were an orcish thief who whispered all the time because they didn't want to be found. Great idea around the table, terrible in the recording process. You have no idea how much noise a glass water bottle makes until you hear it every thirty seconds in a recording. Unless everyone has their own mic, even just hearing the players equally is not easy.

Your friends are not performers. You are not a performer. Even just sitting back and playing some Minecraft on a stream ends up being a tiring process, actually performing a character consistently for several hours is more than a strain. Trust me, I have a whole YouTube channel filled with videos that are absolute garbage. Understanding that performing takes a lot of effort and doing such a thing consistently is a serious energy drain. You may be super invested in your concept, wanting to really drive this mission of performing on a stream or podcast, but that might not be equally shared by your friends who agree to help.

Any podcast or stream that starts today has to compete with paid, fully qualified performers with budgets and direction well beyond the scope of what most "at-home" gamemasters can afford. If you are going to undertake such an endeavour please be aware that the expectations of such a group are somewhat higher than they were even just 5 years ago. That being said, if you do have a group of like minded performance-willing friends, by all means give it a shot.

Activity - Voice Acting Practice

Whilst most of the time I personally find voice acting in role-playing games super cringey at best, and borderline racist at worst, there has become an expectation that this may be a part of what you do in a stream or podcast now. I thought I would include some vocal training to help you come up with a variety of unique voices. This can be used whether you plan to stream or not, but if you are looking at having players act out characters here are some things to consider to help them differentiate their voices, or even just the voices of your numerous NPCs.

Consider how you can combine the following ideas to produce a unique and interesting voice. Keep in mind all of these are scales and by combining one idea with another you can make something truly unique.

- **Light vs Strong** - Do you talk delicately like an elf or bold like a dwarf.
- **Direct vs Indirect** - Do the words you choose get straight to the point or do you beat around the bush.
- **Sudden vs Sustained** - Are your words short and sharp, or do you draaaaag theeeem out maaaan?

By combining these 3 scales you can create the various different "Laban Efforts," a concept known to actors. Other scales to consider might be:

- Nasal vs Regular vs Throaty
- Breathy vs Dry
- Young vs Old
- Masculine vs Feminine
- Fast vs Slow
- Loud vs Soft
- Clear vs Slurred

Take all of these ideas and come up with a variety of voices that you can repeat consistently. This can be a great way to add a bit of a unique experience for your players at your table. You don't need hundreds of voices (although simply playing with the above ideas has the potential to generate millions) just a handful of consistently different and entertaining voices will be enough to get you by.

(**Bonus Activity** - In your daily life see how many times a month you can identify a Jim Cummings voiced character on television shows, movies and games. (Minsc, Hondo Ohnaka, Winnie the Pooh, Tigger, Imhotep, soooo many more.)

Activity - Reflection of Gaming Sessions

As mentioned, Your gaming sessions are probably actually not suitable for liveplay recordings. There will be many things you have to edit out. Next time you are running a game or playing in a game I want you to take a note of how many times the following things happen:

- "**Dead air**" i.e., no one is talking, awkward pauses, the room goes quiet;
- "**Peaks and Spikes**" i.e., any sudden uptake in volume, high pitched noises, rustles of chips, paper, dice hitting tables, glass, metal, birds, dogs, cats, fans, phones, etc;
- "**Fumbles**" i.e., any time people talk over one another, do not pronounce/enunciate words clearly, get tongue tied, repeat words or phrases within the same block of talking, use low-modality words like things and stuff rather than clear direct phrases;
- "**Adult content**" i.e. swearing, gore, violence, threatening behaviour, sexual content, words or phrases that are not politically correct or that are derogatory in nature, bullying or harassment;
- "**Off topic**" i.e., any time the game suddenly or randomly goes to something not game related, this could also be descriptions by the gamemaster or player that make reference to other texts, any time something is described not in direct language but instead as a reference to something else, reference to memes, random non-game related discussions, chat about their day or mutual friends etc;
- "**Background Noise**" i.e., anytime something in the background would be picked up on audio or visual were this recorded, players just chatting and joking and having fun, the fridge opening, closing or humming, cars outside, neighbours with loud music, vibrations from silent phones, noise in other rooms, etc.

Reflect on whether or not recording that particular group

would actually produce a professional quality recording. Even if they were all aware they were acting for a recording, could they stay on topic, not munch snacks, deliver consistently when speaking, prevent themselves from getting excited in the heat of the game? How much content will you have to edit out if you were to record and distribute this? Could it be broadcast live? Is your game mastering even up to scratch for a professional stream? Chances are that most of these questions are going to come up as a "not a good idea to record" response. That does not mean that you can't do it, it just means that it is an issue that will have to be overcome should you attempt to go ahead with such a recording.

Legal Concerns

Okay, so you have a group of friends who are okay at performing and totally fine with you recording them for profit. You get your gear all set up and are ready to start streaming your live-play games on twitch. Maybe you even have a handful of viewers who are friends and family. Everything is going swimmingly, and thanks to an outstanding piece of acting by one of your players your group gets a donation through twitch. It might only be a dollar but at least it is a start right? Isn't that awesome? Okay, so who gets to keep that money? Is it going to be split? Do you as the game master and stream host get it? Does the player who did the acting get it? Does it get split evenly? What about that one player/performer who was away this week when the donation came in, do they get a cut? Suddenly the waters get a lot muddier when money is involved.

There are of course many ways around this. Perhaps you have a legal representative write a contract up about how profits will be split. What exactly constitutes a profit? You paid for the microphones and webcams, the electricity and internet connection. Does that have to be paid first before profit gets split? Or maybe you pay your players a flat fee per episode. The flat fee sounds great at first, but what happens when you don't make any donations for the first 5 sessions and now you as the game master are not just out of pocket but running at a cumulative loss. What if you pay them a flat fee and end up super successful, becoming lucky enough to be one of those $20,000 a year streamers. What about profits from vods uploaded to YouTube and subsequent advertising benefits? Regardless of the methodology of splitting the profits, what about taxes? When do you start having to pay them on stream donations? Does each of your players now have to declare that income as well? Are you now considered an employer by the laws of your country and as such are there now legal responsibilities you have to uphold according to industrial relations law?

Now we are in a legal and financial minefield of our own creation. Any time we add money to group dynamics not only do you get hurt feelings but you also get legal responsibilities that must be dealt with. Unless you are very capable at handling such an operation you could find yourself in some hot water. It is important to consider all these kinds of issues prior to getting the gang together to start streaming or podcasting. If this is a route you are considering then this needs to be discussed clearly with everyone involved and agreements have to be made. Not just verbal agreements either, legally binding contracts. If it is not written down and admissible, did it really even happen?

Copyright, Consequences and Cold Hard Facts

This is just the tip of the legal iceberg. Assuming that you get all that sorted and do have outstanding friendship groups who are also happy to legally bind themselves to your operation through contracts, what exactly is your stream or podcast going to look/sound like? When we make resources for our online games at home there is no onus to ensure copyright laws are followed. The most public and obvious example of this kind of issue is the ongoing legal battles that streamers are having regarding playing games and music on their streams. DMCA strikes are a real and potentially expensive thing to deal with. As a person who has tried to upload his live play of Borderlands onto YouTube, I can tell you that even just the music in the background of a gameplay experience is enough to get you into hot water with the copyright holders of the world. The musical choices you make, the graphics and artworks you use, the maps and tokens, and even the modules and monsters you use are all subject to copyright law.

Here is a very simple example that you may not be aware of: You are not allowed to publish any material that demonstrates Dungeons and Dragons 5th Edition gameplay containing monsters that are not included in the SRD (System Reference Document); *Beholders, Mind Flayers, Kuo-Toa, Slaad, Umber-Hulks, Yuan-ti,* and so many more are all staple creatures that simply are not allowed in published materials. Does your live-play game recording count towards that potential copyright issue? This is a legally dubious area. Does your live-play game recording include any way for an audience member to learn the statistics of those monsters? Say their HP, attacks, damage? Is that inferable through what is said and published by you? Does that count as publishing that information? The truth is that the law does not have an official definition for such a thing given we are in such new territory. You may be using tokens or showing artworks of such things. These appearing in your stream are legally publications of such artwork, technically speaking. Do you have the right to use those images? You commissioned stock art or maybe even drew the picture of the beholder yourself, you say, well then you are in breach of the copyright tied to that creature. Even something in the SRD, like a Goblin, can be considered too close to the trademarks of Paizo in their Pathfinder Roleplaying Game; a fact that I know because Red Goblin Games got a cease and desist letter for when they began publishing content. Red Goblin Games had to completely redesign their logo and republish all their books because of the infringement. As you can see, legally this is a very precarious situation and as the law is still catching up with the developing technology it is a risk that is hard to navigate.

All of these copyright issues and we haven't even started to discuss the idea of using published modules for live gameplay, or character creation (which is also forbidden to be discussed in 'published materials' by the open game licence) or a myriad of other potential speed humps on the road. Who owns the characters? Imagine you are very successful and at some point one of your players decides to go off and start their own little business. Can they use the character they played? Can you use it in merchandising? Did you put that in your contract when you wrote it? Looking at the comics industry we can see that this is still a sticky subject that is yet to be completely determined. Even with contracts in place, legally speaking, there are many examples which can be seen where creators and publishers are at odds and contracts can be overturned. Who owns the likeness of your players? George Lucas included such a clause in his contracts with all the Star Wars actors back in the day. Does that mean your players can't themselves stream without infringing on the contract you created? Or if they didn't include that are you allowed to profit from their likeness in merchandise? Anyway, I think that demonstrates that things are not cut and dry when it comes to legal concerns. It takes more than just the intention to do things right by everyone, especially once money gets involved. All I am saying is to start considering this well before you start becoming successful.

Activity - Interviews

If you are considering following this route, why not do some research with streamers who already do what it is you want to do. Get in contact with some streamers and ask if you can interview them to find out how they deal with these kinds of things. This is a great idea for just in general gaining an understanding of what is involved behind the scenes anyway. Obviously the big streams are probably not going to have the time or ability to communicate with you on this level, but there are many smaller streamers and podcasts that may be happy to find the time. If you are in fan groups you might be able to get in contact with them via social media, otherwise track them down directly. The Cyberpunk Uncensored discord group/facebook group are an excellent and friendly bunch of people who might be able to help here. As are many of the D&D based roleplaying podcasts out there who are happy to have fan conversations as well. The Call of Cthulhu groups I am involved with on facebook also have been great places to get research like this answered.

Before you organise an interview, make a list of questions you want answered. Go in prepared. See if any of that information is available for free already. You might be surprised what you can already find out just by looking at their twitch account page or personal websites.

Growing Audiences

Let's say you have worked things out and do decide to make a podcast/stream your game. You get everyone together, do a few practice runs, and end up getting your game going. You start playing weekly and are on twitch at the same time every week. But the views are still at 1. What do you do now? Growing an audience is one of the hardest parts of producing content of any kind. And more than just having a number of followers, you actually want engaged and receptive members of your community who will support you, not just randoms who scroll past your content.

Being Consistent

Step one to getting a following of any calibre is to be consistent. If you can't even post regular content how will an audience know when to look for your work. Reducing the barrier to entry is a big part of this. When it comes to podcasts and streaming, if you actually do manage to develop a loyal following, they will want to build their community off the back of your content. Things like spoilers, plot twists and even just chatting about the latest episode is something that can bring a community together. If we know a podcast is going to drop on a certain day as fans we can be ready for it. If you want fans to talk about your games in your community groups you don't want someone logging in to find a meme or comment that spoils what happened in the episode beforehand just because you streamed in an inconsistent manner.

Posting consistently is an exercise in managing expectations and feeding social buzz. A good way to deal with this is to create content in a batch ahead of time and release it on a consistent basis. Planning things well will give you a buffer zone and that can make a big difference. Whilst it is true that we no longer live in a society where people gather around a television at a certain time to watch their weekly shows, having a "timeslot" when things are released can give an element of structure and consistency which many of the fans will need if you are going to keep them on board. It allows you to tell them when things will come out and it also allows you to manipulate them with memes, comments and content to hype them up before a stream etc. Dropping some teasers for what is coming throughout the week can remind people to listen/watch and it can be a really fun way to engage your community.

Activity - Scheduling
Over the next 3 months take a diary/phone calendar and mark every day you have something to do. This includes going to work, visiting family, doing the shopping, seeing a movie, visiting your gaming shop, etc. Plot down your time. Also note down times when you have come home and just felt exhausted and do not want to do anything.

After three months of doing this accurately, go back through and highlight with 2 colours. Highlight in a red or pink colour the things that are set in stone, that absolutely must be done. Work, church, family, etc. Also include in red/pink the times you felt tired. And in a green or blue colour highlight things which could be spent doing a stream instead. Get a clear visual on a calendar just when you would realistically be able to add a regular game with 100% certainty.

Being accurately aware of your time is important. Streaming and podcasting is a full time commitment if you want to actually succeed at it. Do you honestly have enough time to do something regularly? The second part of this is asking if your "actors" also have this amount of time.

Adding Value

One of the big reasons people just don't care about your podcast or stream is because it doesn't really add any value. If it is just a bunch of folks sitting around a table with a mic that can hardly hear two-thirds of them properly, and a bunch of crinkly crisp eating noises, and slurping of drinks, and tapping on tables as people play with their dice, then chances are it's going to be a major turn-off for most viewers/listeners. Your game should be more than just a live play game if it is going to be fun.

One basic way of doing this is adding bells and whistles to the game; graphics, sound effects, editing, etc. Whilst this is generally what people think of when they are talking about adding value I would argue that these "fireworks" are often a lot of effort and usually create more problems to go wrong. A great example of this is the Cybernation Uncensored podcast. I love these guys and listen regularly. They are sponsored by Syrinscape, an audio environment suite that gives you sound effects for ambient sound. Whilst this can help fill dead air on their podcast it also often can be a distraction, being a little too loud or repetitive and this is something that annoys the hell out of me and makes me have to switch podcasts half way through.

A far better way to add value is how you would add value for your players anyway, through storytelling and character development. People who are going to be an audience for a podcast or stream are there because they want that character/lore interaction. They want to experience characters growing and exploring their differences. This is why we get attached to good books and television shows. Take for instance A Game of Thrones. Many people were very hooked on both the books and shows of that series, not because it is such a well made production but because we grew attached to the ideals and personalities of the characters.

If you are going to run adventures in roleplaying games as a stream or podcast it has to be more than just hack and slash the monsters. All the really successful streams have bold characters who are all different from each other. They aren't the "stereotypical" [insert class here]. They are really unique twists on those with their own motivations and storylines, or if they are the stereotype then they are super exaggerated to create a satirical version of the archetype. Telling an enthralling story is a big part of adding value and it is something you can easily do as a game master with a bit of prep and work with your players.

Looking at Competition

Look at what is already out there. These days streams are competing with some really high end production values. Now not everyone is going to expect huge studios with celebrity guests and voice actors, but just be aware that some chumps around the table burping sodas and munching chips just simply won't cut it if you want to be a performer. You are trying to build a brand and appear professional and a great way to see how that is done well is to view people in your space that are already doing this.

Are you aware of other streams or podcasts? More than just your favourites! Go and see all different levels of this sphere and see what amatuer productions look like and what the pros are doing. Take notes on the production, not the content. What format are they using? How are they embellishing their production and where? Is this something that you like or dislike?

The goal here is not to copy and paste but to analyse and inspire. As mentioned above one trend seems to be the increase in super cringey voice acting in podcasts and streams now thanks to critical role. Whilst I can see how this adds an element that was previously missing it is not the kind of thing that I appreciate. If I were to start a stream I would not be adopting this, but that would be a deliberate choice. I would be aware that there is an expectation that this happens in other places and that said expectation would have to be addressed. In many ways I may need to compensate for that in other areas.

You can not make a good business in performance without being aware what other options for entertainment people have out there. Looking at the competition is an important step to defining what you are going to do yourself and also what you are going to do to make your performance different.

Activity - Research and Value-add
Make a list of things you can value-add by looking at your competitors. What are people currently adding to their stream productions? Also make a list of things people are adding that you want to avoid. Having these lists will help you to define your stream/podcast. Once you have a list of 30 or 40 things you are going to do/not do, look at what these have in common. Take some time to write a short paragraph or two that helps define your brand and style. Consider this a kind of mission statement or "about page" for the podcast you are considering starting.

Dealing with Trolls

If you put anything on the internet you are going to get criticism and feedback that is not positive. Nowhere is this more apparent than during live streaming such as on twitch and YouTube. As someone who tried streaming on twitch when it first came out I am very aware of this. There is nothing as haunting as realising that once you get a dedicated troll there is little you can do to stop them from causing grief on your stream. Banning and silencing etc only works if they only have a single account. Most of these griefers will have more than one, or can easily make multiple with the click of a few buttons.

I have very clear and distinct memories of my wife and I playing on twitch having a great time and just a few people saying some rude comments which entirely derailed our night. Now that I have a family I am aware that doing public things draws attention to my loved ones as well. Someone releasing my address is also releasing the address of my family. Someone watching my stream and seeing my children can make threats against those children which I have to take seriously and have little recourse to deal with. It can be a very unhappy invasion of privacy which upon analysis the performer has to realise they actually invited in by asking to be a public figure.

On the one hand, if you have done your homework and built a strong and solid community then usually they will take care of the trolls for you. But when you are just starting out, this is not something you can count on. My policy was always "Ban early, ban often." Set clear rules and if those rules are broken I would come down with harsh punishments. I generally give any individual an honest chance to make a mistake. "We don't do that here and if you keep it up we might have to boot you buddy." was a common phrase. Usually people see you are serious and if they are legit making a mistake it's not a drama but if they are 'griefing' they will keep testing those waters. Like a toddler or a teenager what they are actually testing is your willingness to follow through with a boundary. Don't disappoint them and do follow through.

One final word on trolls online. Be aware that they are seeking a reaction/attention. If you give it to them they win. Whilst I will give a warning once, I won't make a big deal about a ban. Just ban quietly and move on with your life. The more you make a big deal out of it the more they will poke the bear. Try not to take what they say personally because they are trying to provoke you. You have to have a thick skin and a good sense of humour.

Activity - Rules
Make a list of specific rules that will be the rules of your stream. You want no more than 10 rules, but these must cover every expectation you have clearly. "Don't be a dick" whilst a great phrase is a rule that is not specific. You must have clear behaviour expectations for your stream and they should be on your channels page. The same is true for any area where you are coordinating a mass group of people, be it a discord server, forum or even just facebook page.

A Realistic Expectation

It is important to set a realistic expectation for you. Quite realistically, no matter what social media you are engaging with, be it Facebook, Twitch, YouTube, Instagram etc. setting a realistic expectation for what kinds of interactions you should expect is important. A really popular social media channel will be lucky if it has a 20% reach, a 10% engagement rate and a 0.1% click through to sales rate. That means that for every 1,000 followers you have you will likely get less than 1 of them actually following your call to action. This doesn't matter if the call to action is something that is free or paid. There are certainly things you can do to increase this, but realistically on average this is a high number for what to expect. Chances are that many of your followers will have been picked up over time and are simply not even seeing your content because of how algorithms filter out content. Of the few that do see it, chances are that more than half are just going to scroll by and ignore it, consuming it passively.

Of those that do actually pay attention and aren't zombies to it, very few of them are actually going to get off their butts and do what you ask them to do. This is just the nature of the game we are playing. As such a lot of what we do is about saturation of that market to try and increase the number of opportunities you have to reach any individual.

Also be aware that it takes time to grow a channel. If you want 100 followers/subscribers you are going to have to have 1,000 streams/videos. If you want 1,000 followers/subscribers you may need close to 50,000 stream hours under your belt. It does not happen fast if it is organic.

Chapter 6 - Blogging/Podcasting Content

Whilst the most public and popular method of streaming and podcasting seems to be live play games, another avenue does exist for the keen podcaster or streamer. It also opens up other avenues such as blogging or vlogging, which has shown to be very powerful as a moneymaker in the past. This method sees the content creator make content that is not game play but instead reflecting on the actual games, products and state of the hobby in general. Content Blogging is an ever growing industry and actually has the potential for more upsells. Whilst it is harder to grow an audience with a content blog/channel/podcast the effort required is less and the possibility of pushing sales is more.

Regularity of Content

The first thing that you must come to terms with is the idea that you need people to return to your content. This means that you must make regularly updated content. Posting regularly, as mentioned before, helps your followers bypass the algorithm and actually see your content. Whether it is podcasting, traditional blogging, video blogging on YouTube or just posting to social media, releasing content at regular and predictable intervals will make your fan base be more likely to engage with your stuff. I post on my instagram and facebook at 6pm Australian Eastern Standard Time every single day. I have short form content and regularly create a whole batch of content and line it up in the planner months ahead. Everyone who follows me knows at dinner time in Australia they can find a new post on their socials from me. I have done this for the past decade almost, be it for Game Masters Stash or for my own Arjade Productions channels.

Why do we need regular content? The answer is that depending on how you monetise, this is where your cash is going to come from. You need people to come back regularly to see your advertisements or updates when you release a new product. If you are a podcast or a vlog on YouTube, you rely on the advertising that is given to your channel to make the money. This means people have to come back to see your new videos as they are released. If they know they can check in on you once a week and see all the new videos in one go then they will do so. If your posts are irregular and they check back and there is nothing there sometimes but then twenty videos there another time, chances are they are going to eventually stop appearing on your views as they go and find someone who publishes more in line with their content consumption expectations.

There is an exception to this, and that is posting of evergreen content. Evergreen content is when a post/article/video contains information that is always something people are looking for. For instance my most popular video on YouTube is "A brief history of Battletech for Beginners." This battletech lore is not something that really changes given it is a historical video. And new players are always coming into the game and need to be caught up. I would encourage you to find ways to slip evergreen content into your regular work so that you can make the most out of both worlds, the trending content and the evergreen.

Activity - Knowing Your Schedule

The first and most important thing for making regular content is to be sure that you will be able to post regularly. Here is what I want you to do. Decide on some content you would like to make regularly. Maybe it's statting a monster or making a magic item or coming up with a backstory for an NPC. You decide something that will take you 10 minutes or so to put together. Pick that one thing, and then for the next 3 months I want you to pick a consistent time in the day where you believe you will have both a free 10 minutes and the energy and creativity to do that one thing you chose to do. And for the next 3 months I want you to try and do that one thing at that one time every single day. Write it in a google docs document or save it into a folder or something and just collect it. Don't publish it anywhere, just collect it. Every day you do not create content, make this down on a calendar. After 3 months you will see a pattern emerge of just how many days of posts you actually can do, realistically, in your schedule. Work out how many days a week is sustainable for you in all honesty. Then I want you to minus 1 to that many days, just in case. If the number of days is more than zero, that is your schedule for posting. If the days are less than zero you simply do not have the time to post regularly once a day.

One thing I saw a lot of at Game Master Stash was people agreeing to post more than they could fit into their schedule. We would often get content writers who simply couldn't keep up with what they agreed to. It wasn't that we demanded they post a certain amount, just that they post on the days they said they would. With the exception of just 3 long term posters (one of which was myself), not a single admin was able to keep up with the schedule. The problem was not keeping up with the schedule but the psychological impact that came with not posting. If you missed a day, you felt guilty, and that would make it harder to post the next day, and the more of those built up the more terrible the admins who were missing days felt. If they had just agreed to do less days then they would have missed fewer posts and actually ended up posting more frequently. The same is true for you. Set a goal that is achievable. If you have more time to post, see the below activity.

Activity - Build Up a Stockpile

So if you did the previous activity you will now have a crap load of posts saved somewhere on a google drive, your phone or whatever. If you do not, then go back and do that activity. Having a stockpile helps you to keep your posts up. It gives you a buffer zone. Having now made whatever posts you have been working on, be it social posts, blog entries, podcast snippets etc, you should have enough to schedule in the planner of whatever distribution method you are planning to do. So go and schedule it. Try to keep up with your schedule from the previous activity (whatever that final schedule ended up being) and on the "minus 1" day mentioned, if you have time, spend that day making extra content as a backup in case you need it. You can also spend that day doing maintenance on your social media/blog/whatever, responding to comments, promoting it on reddits or in facebook groups, making advertising content or looking for sponsors. With a stockpile that is of a reasonable size, you gain breathing room so that you do not need to feel pressure to post every single day. Sometimes just doing double or triple posting to give yourself a head start when busy times are around the corner can be a real blessing. Definitely try to do this.

If you are planning to do long form content, say reviews or podcasts, try to have five or six fully edited posts ready to go just in case of emergency. Maybe your work gets busy or your family has a crisis. Doing this will give you peace of mind.

What Do People Want to Read/Hear

Great, so you decided you are going to make content. Can you just pump out any old garbage and hope they lap it up? No. The big problem if you want to be successful is making content people actually want. This is quite a complicated issue so to explain it better let us look at a few examples from my time at Game Master Stash.

At The Stash, we would regularly post NPCs. This was probably our main bread and butter in terms of posts. Many admins who would sign up to write NPCs would write these great amazing characters. They would have crazy long back stories and in-depth personalities. This was part of the reason why many admins had trouble keeping up with posts, actually. The depth of effort they put into their characters was huge and as such was unsustainable. Then they would post these NPCs up and see a medium amount of interaction. Why? Because these great overarching stories, whilst creative and beautiful to read, were not something Game Masters could take to their games and use. What GMs needed was simple background characters, not mighty heroes who steal the spotlight from their players. So whenever we would post NPCs who were simple farmers or traders who had a single interesting gimmick they would see a lot more engagement from our GMs.

Another example is the opposite of this, Random Generators.

One of the more meme-able content that we made at The Stash was the Random Generator, where you would take your birthday and name and use those things to create some kind of character, magic item, or other randomly gimmicked thing. These random generators were great because we could then take your information and use it to steal your identity and rob your bank account. (That last sentence is a joke specifically for Garrett and Luke if you are reading. For legal reasons I want to make it clear that we did not do this despite the insistence of many comments saying we did.) The real reason these generators were great is because they are interactive, fun and shareable. As such they get insanely good engagement. However, if you do them too often people stop responding. So what would often happen is that new admins would see how much engagement they would get with one of these and then just spam them every week for a while. As a result people would stop caring and our overall page numbers would dip. If you go to the well too often, then the water dries up.

Finally, sometimes when a new product would be released we might make content that was tied to that product. Perhaps a new book of magic items was coming out so we would put out some magic items in the style of that to try and grab onto that trend. This content would usually do okay, but at the end of the day no one would come back to that very trend-chasey content. When was the last time that you went back to see what happened to Hanson (singers of the hit song MmmBop!) chances are you haven't thought about them in quite some time. Or when was the last time you kept up with who the latest ALS Icebucket Challenge celebrity is. I'm again guessing not recently, right? Chasing tends is one way to get some engagement, but it's a hamster wheel of never ending frustration. It isn't sustainable.

You have to think about what people actually need. Do they need a 30 minute long webcam recording of you whinging about the state of the game? Probably not. Do they need a well made battle report to keep them entertained and help new players learn the game? Yes they absolutely do. Do they need a review of upcoming products? Probably, yes so that they can make decisions about if they are going to buy it. Do they need a meme reel where you make potentially racist, homophobic or misogynist comments "as a joke" to try and get views? Probably not. Which of these content ideas are sustainable? Which of these content ideas are evergreen? Finding what your audience really needs is hard, but you will know it when you see it. Just remember to think like an audience member, not like a content creator.

Activity - Make a List and Check it Twice

Now that you are thinking about the kinds of posts that you want to be making, taking some time to actually just make a list of post ideas can really help give some structure to your content. I know it seems counter intuitive taking time to write about posts rather than writing the actual posts, but you will find that this is time well spent. One day, sit down for 30 minutes to an hour and just think about the kinds of posts you can make. This can be an open-book (or open-phone) research task where you are looking at the ideas being posted by other accounts in your sphere. I will often do this, just sit down and think "what have I not posted a lot of, how can I make that better?" The other place that I often get inspiration is looking at posts outside my niche. What are they doing in the world of authors? What are they doing in the world of entrepreneurship? What are they doing in the world of wrestling, or movies, or skateboarding, or esports? What kinds of posts are other creators making that could apply to the realm of the hobby gamer? Once you start looking for "content ideas" rather than just "content" you will find that the list will outgrow the amount of time you have to actually make the posts. It then becomes a matter of choosing what path works best by removing ideas rather than struggling to come up with them.

Chapter 7 - Chasing the Social Media Dragon

Regardless of what you choose to do, chances are at some point you are going to need to engage with some kind of social media to get the word out there about your stuff. Gone are the days of "Email lists" and static blog addresses. Don't get me wrong, Email lists are still the best way to send promotions to your followers, and static blogs are great if you have the ability to bring traffic to them. Generally speaking, people don't want to go to their content, they want the content to come to them. As such getting some kind of following on Social Media is going to be key. Be warned though, it is like a drug addiction and if you aren't careful you may find yourself spending all your time managing your social media account and not making any products/services which you can then use to make money. Having followers and likes on stuff is great but if you aren't using that audience to generate cash why are you even doing it?

Growing a Following

How you grow a following, like everything in this book, is a complicated process where there is no real straight up formula to achieve it. Posting regularly, posting stuff that is relevant, engaging with your community in an authentic and positive way, these things will all make a difference. Growing a following takes time and patience and most importantly a bit of luck.

With The Stash we had 1,000 followers when I started, and then just thanks to posting regularly we ended up at 17,000 followers when I took my leave to focus on Arjade Productions. What did we do to gain that many people? Simply posting every day for years. Occasionally sharing our content to a few facebook groups and reddit pages. How many of those fans went on to buy products from Arjade? Very few. There is a difference between engaged followers and passive followers and you kind of need both.

If you have just 100 loyal and engaged followers you can make a business for yourself. This is true in any niche or industry. With 100 loyal and engaged followers you can get them to share and promote your work and do a lot of the heavy growing for you. But obtaining those followers is not easy. This is where luck comes in.

Many younger people try clout chasing and trend following, but all they are doing essentially is buying themselves passive followers. Passive followers used to be great because you could go to sponsors and say "hey, look I have 17,000 followers" and they would give you a deal. Now though most companies are onto this and will follow up with questions like "what is your engagement rate, what is your click through rate, how many other sponsors have done business with you and what were the results?" Whilst having that big number looks very impressive and encourages the algorithms to show your content to other new potential followers, it does nothing for generating your income. Buying followers or "doing a give away" has the same effect. It might give you a bump in the short term but it hurts you in the long run.

To get a consistently growing following you must post regularly and promote community. This means actually being engaged as a follower of other similarly sized members of your niche. Having a good content strategy also doesn't hurt.

Content Strategies

It is one thing to make content that you post regularly. It is another thing to have a clear strategy with what you are planning to do with it. If you are making this content then it should be leading somewhere. Perhaps you can collate it into a collected works, a book of some kind that you can sell. Maybe you are just doing it to get the interest of the followers and get them on your side.

Many marketers will tell you a good content strategy is the 80-20 method, where 80% of your content is fun and engaging and useful stuff and 20% is trying to push the hard sell. In my experience this is way too much 20 and not enough 80. From what I have seen, more like a 95-5 method is more accurate. These days you need the bulk of your content as stuff that people will interact with just so that you can get over the algorithm's hurdles. This is very arbitrary and dependent on the niche. If you are an artist making copyright infringing fan art then you may find that 80-20 is about right. Likewise if you are a gym dude-bro selling protein shakes this may also be more in that range. If you are an author or game creator like myself you really need that 5% critical hit range just to keep people coming back to your site and not unfollowing.

How often to post is also a controversial topic. This also is very much dependent on platform and niche. When I was at The Stash I was very confident that posting more than once every 4 hours was impacting our reach. I said this on multiple occasions. Sure enough, on the days when people "forgot" to post and there were only 2 posts we would often get a reach of 1,700-5,000 views and on days where everyone remembered to post and our 4 posts went out the views on each post would often not break 300-500 in the first 24 hours. YouTube videos are a similar concept. If you post them all at once often not many get shown to your audience, but once every 4 days seems to be about the correct amount. Again, this is where evergreen, searchable content comes in.

When to post once again is a whole essay-able topic, but let's put it this way. Think about your target audience and when they are using the app you are on. Meal times/commute times is the most successful time to post. That and toilet breaks, but since the call of nature comes differently to everyone it is harder to plan for. I try to post around dinner time, because I know that is when I myself stare into my nightmare rectangle and watch the world burn, so I assume others do too.

Finally and I guess most importantly WHAT to post is the big question on many people's lips. As mentioned above I think it is important to post regular, relevant content that builds community rather than toxicity. I like to try to post evergreen content at least 5% of the time. I try to post fun, sharable content at least 5% of the time and I like to post heartbreakingly emotional content 1% of the time to just remind people that I can be a good writer haha. Tutorials are also often some of my most engaged with products. Writing guides or how tos generally get good reach and also eventually aggregate into writing a book at some point. I also like to write actually usable content.

A lot of what I do write is written in bulk and is generally sub par at the minute, mostly because I am trying to work on bigger things rather than growing my audience. Once I have a catalogue and a functioning website it is my plan to push my own socials even further and I guess this really is more or a key issue. Why are you growing your following? Until you have a range of products to push on them, growing the fan base doesn't really do anything but eat into your product development time. Which brings us nicely to the next section of this chapter.

Where's the Money, Lebowski?

It is all well and good to have 100 loyal fans promoting your work, but if you aren't benefiting from this then why the heck are you doing it all. You have to have a plan to monetise your work. Posting YouTube Shorts will jack up your followers and view time super quick, but it is not advertised so you don't get any ad revenue from that. It is counter productive. Posting every day is all well and good, but to what end? You are here reading this because you want to make money right? So where is the money, Lebowski?

Advertising

The most obvious advertising you are going to be doing is advertising your own products. Hopefully you have a large enough catalogue of products that you can make some sales every time you advertise. This is not currently true for me, but we do pretty well making a handful of sales each month. At this stage I am making roughly $30-100 a month from the sales of my gaming content that is out there. Every time I release a new product this amount grows, and the plan is to continue to develop my catalogue. Looking at me you will also notice that most of my products are small-yield, meaning that the sales do not yield much in profits, selling for $5 or less to make more sales. When I produce higher quality products the yield will also increase. I know many other content makers who bring in closer to $1,000 per month because they have a more developed catalogue and are able to advertise to a larger audience when they release products. You will probably be pushing your own product, hopefully about 5% or less of the time and hopefully that earns you some revenue. This revenue will grow the more products you have to advertise and the larger your advertising base is.

Other ways to milk this are to get some paid advertising going for your socials. YouTube and Podcasts have their own ways of incorporating Google AdSense into their views, as does traditional blogging. You might even be lucky enough to get some paid spots, like Raid Shadow Legends or Raycon Earbuds. Just be aware that you should read every contract you sign up for and know just how you are meant to be getting paid. Some of these are an amazing rip off and not worth your time, others can be consistent breadwinners. Do your research. If you do want to find paid sponsors there are places to look for them and I would encourage you to find someone who is more skilled than I at doing that to guide you through it. Also be aware of the legal requirements if you do have a sponsored ad in your content as some platforms require that this be denoted clearly for legal reasons. Personally I think that is just an ethical thing to do regardless but be warned there are legal ramifications if you fail to do this in some instances.

Affiliate Marketing

Affiliate Marketing is where you find a link to a product which you then try to push on your customers. It is basically commission work, requiring you to make a sale in order to harvest a finders fee. Some affiliate marketing deals will tie you to their account regardless of product purchased though those are few and far between these days. Many YouTubers and instagramers use affiliate marketing and it is a common way to get some side cash. You have to make sure you stand behind the products you are marketing however or you will actually be tying yourself to a reputation of garbage quality. In one example of this, there was a brand of popular health supplements that many influencers were pushing back in 2012. It was later revealed that those supplements contained a very, very large quantity of rat faeces and the company got shut down. In a surprise to no one, that month in 2012 one of the trending topics was "I'm sorry, I didn't mean to sell you rat poop," and many of those influencers are not making content today.

Pushing Products

Every month or so I get a message from some random person and the message goes something like this. "Hey, you look like you fit our brand. I can tell you [insert random flattery here] and we think you would be a great fit for our line of [insert product here]. If you respond to [some instagram/facebook page that is not actually this person] and tell them you were contacted by [name of this recruiter] they will help you get started making money selling our products today!" And basically I delete these. They are cold calling pyramid schemes but on social media sites instead of in person. If I wanted to sell AVON I would just sell avon, rather than get involved in some random multi-level marketing scheme with people in another country that I am unlikely to ever meet.

You, on the other hand, may be tempted to give this kind of thing a go. Often the products that come my way are often clothing brands, jewellery brands or health supplements. If that fits your niche of social media influence then you may consider giving these a try. The way these companies say they work is that you buy products at 70% off and then sell them on to your followers and keep the difference. The way the companies actually work is that they encourage idiots on the internet to buy their goods, telling them they are getting a huge discount, and then they don't care whether that product gets sold on or not because they have already made their money. Their goal is to shift their inventory to you to deal with for a price that makes them profit regardless. If you want a box full of clothes in different sizes, by all means give it a try haha.

That being said, with the right kind of social media design you could easily use something like this, (or what I would do is go to AliExpress and buy the same jewellery myself to stock a shop) and then create an online store of related side hustle wares. You can then try to push this product with your own posts and have a good time with it.

Activity - Investigate Monetisation Strategies
Have a look at the social media accounts you currently follow. As you are scrolling through over the next month or so, take note of the different ways people are trying to use the nightmare rectangle to capitalise. Do any of these feel like something you could copy? Do any of these make you cringe and feel like you wouldn't feel comfortable doing them? Are any of these actually doing something they aren't saying they are doing? Take the time to think about just how your favourite influencers are making money and try to figure out how you could replicate that for yourself.

Chapter 8 - Conventions

Something unique to nerd culture is the concept of getting everyone who is interested in a particular nerdy pursuit together in one location to celebrate as a commercial event. The Gaming Convention is a huge resource for the money master because it's one of the only times where your audience is all under one roof. It is also a great way to build a profile for yourself and get your name out there. Be aware though that it is a real jerk move to only attend a convention as a gamemaster for the purposes of boosting your sales and event coordinators are aware that this is often what people do. If you want to get asked back again next year you have to be authentic and really want to be there for reasons other than the cash grab. There are many ways you can interact with a convention, be it as a game master running endorsed games, as a stall amongst many in the marketplace, or as some kind of fan that engages with the convention to its fullest.

Who Gets Chosen to Run

One of the bigger problems with the plan of running games at conventions is that there is a limit as to who gets to run and what they get to run. You may be hoping to run your latest module or something in your personal campaign setting but chances are that if you are lucky enough to be asked to run they might have something in mind for you already. Often convention coordinators will want to hear what your plan is and see if it fits with their vibe. They also want to ensure that you are a GM capable of engaging with the kinds of folks you meet at a convention.

Convention games are very different, as mentioned in previous sections. There are a great deal of expectations. You also have to be an advocate for the convention as well as yourself. Your behaviour is representing the convention as a whole and as such how you react to situations is reflective of the corporate structures behind you. How you handle delicate issues, problem players, murderhoboing, descrimination both from players or in game, political discussion or even just general rudeness all will impact how the organisers of the event see you and if they are happy with your performance.

In addition to this you will have to be able to run the kind of game that is going to suit everyone who attends. Conventions are a really unique setting where you will be overwhelmed by the diversity of random players. If you want to be chosen to run again in the future you will have to develop the ability to engage these kinds of random people.

Sometimes conventions are desperate for hosts. In this case you might scrape by one year or two being a bad game master. But at some stage that will no longer be the case and there will be an awkward conversation to be had. Being mindful of your own performance and attitudes is key to success as a public game master.

The opposite is also true. Often conventions will be very popular and trying to get into one as a game master might be tricky. You may need to prove yourself with a tidy resume of times you have run things in the past. You might have to be prepared for an interview where they want to test your approaches to problem players.

Activity - Prepare For a Convention Interview.
Take a moment to think about the following questions and prepare yourself for getting interviewed on the spot. These are just a few of the many potential questions a convention host might ask you if you want to run at a big convention.

- What are your strengths as a game master?
- What are some of your areas of improvement as a game master?
- Can you think of a time where you had player conflict in a game? How did you resolve it?
- Can you think of a time where created something really exciting with a group of players? Tell us more about that.
- Imagine this scenario, you have been selected to run a game for the convention and as you are preparing your introductions there is one player who has turned up and

brought their friend. Their friend didn't pre-register and the table is full. The player is really desperate to have their friend join in and when you explain the problem they get upset and state that if you won't let their friend play they are going to not play either. How do you handle this scenario?

- What are your strategies to keep the game you are running within the time limit (for example 2 hours) and running on time?
- Have you ever ran for a group of larger than 12 players? How did that go and what are some strategies you used as a game master?
- Imagine this scenario, You have been running a game for about half an hour now with a group at the convention and all of a sudden one of the players gets a message on their phone. They ask how much longer the game has to run for. After hearing the answer they nod their head and go back to playing. After about five minutes they begin to take a lot more risks with both their characters and the party. They start trying to provoke other characters into arguments, try to steal items from other characters in game, generally start causing problems for the group cohesion. Other players start to show signs that they are not comfortable with this. How do you handle this situation?

The key with answering these questions is to remember player inclusion, fairness, and following any policies the convention might have regarding the rules. A little compassion can also go a long way. Remember any interview is always asking you to demonstrate your capabilities so try to remember the STAR principle (Situation, Task goal, Action taken, Result).

What Gets to Run

In addition to which game masters get chosen, what adventure is also something that is very important to be considered. Often you are looking at a few hour long session between 4-10 strangers who will never see each other again. You will have to be able to run a game conducive to that environment. Knowing what to zoom through and what to engage with will be something that is learnt over time, but you should have practised running some one shots long before you even consider running for a convention. You will find staples like combat and exposition need to be tailored to the situation you are in otherwise they will bog down the story.

What themes and elements are present is also a key feature to consider. You have to appeal to the general public with your story. Anything too controversial or mature might require some kind of warning. As mentioned previously safety tools are a must for a convention game, but ideally you shouldn't be risking anything that would potentially require them.

Activity - Preparing a Convention Dosier
Take some time to prepare a simple one shot adventure for your favourite game that would be suitable for a convention. Generate the adventure and 10 premade characters that would create a balanced party. Do your best to keep things contained, within the story and the time limit. Create all the notes you would require for this adventure and all the handouts required for players. Be sure to include some combat, some social encounters, some puzzles and some ways for players to interact with the strangers that make up their party over the two or three hours that they will be playing. Prepare these and lay them out professionally so that they can be printed and given to a convention organiser to demonstrate your ability to run a game suitable for a convention. Be sure to playtest running the game a few times with these materials, preferably with random play groups, and ensure that things go according to plan.

Volunteering and Converting to Sales

You aren't the first genius who has thought "I know, I will volunteer to run a game and then I can spam players with my sellable items. They will be so enthralled by my game they will absolutely snap it up! Easy money!" and let me tell you right now you are 100% wrong.

First of all, if you do plan to use your game mastering at a convention as a means of promoting yourself, there is nothing wrong with that but make sure you have asked permission from the co-ordinators of the event. There may be rules about how they want those kinds of promotions done. Also it would be a jerk move to just shove your promos down the throats of your players who thought they were just coming for a fun day of games. When I think about this sort of predatory conversion it makes me cringe reflecting on the old days of Games Workshop stores in Australia. I would go in to just buy a box of minis and end up having to deflect the constant upsells they were trying to push on me. I didn't have the money and also I didn't really care. It just made me not want to go in there and be a part of that. This is the opposite of what you want to do if you are trying to promote yourself. By chasing them you will force them away.

Secondly, in my experience it rarely works out the way you are currently envisaging it in your head. Just simply crunching the numbers on this, let's say you run 3 games a day for 3 days of a convention. In each game you get between 4-8 people, and let's average that out to 5 a game for ease of maths. That is a total of 45 people over 3 days that you get to speak to. And whilst you will be spending a solid 3 or 4 hours with those people most of that is being spent playing a game not selling your wares. If we assume 20% of your conversations result in some kind of social media follow, which later turns into say 2% conversion into a sale you are still looking at less than 1 single person actually buying your stuff. And those numbers are super optimistic as it is more likely that it will be 0.2% or less that turn into a sale. If you instead spent your time at a booth or even just roaming the convention talking to people you can easily see 300 people a day, for almost 1,000 people total meaning with the same effort and time and assuming the same super optimistic numbers you'd make 20 sales that day. A far better investment of your time and you didn't piss off the organisers so you will be able to come back next year.

Approach volunteering with the respect it deserves. If you are volunteering to work at a convention, or any kind of event for charity, schools, community, etc., then be sure to remain focussed on the goal of running the game and building community rather than building your business. Being an active member of the gaming community is a healthy thing. Being a predatory used-car-salesman looking to snipe some shmucks is not a healthy thing.

Selling at a Booth

The best way to make profit at a convention is by being a salesperson at a booth. Now this is a complicated topic which we won't go into in a great amount of detail here but know that there are many guides online about how to make money selling at conventions. These include how to set up your shop and how to get the most out of your time there. I thought I would spend some time here talking about what to expect working at a booth.

Vandals and Thieves

From my experience the first thing to expect is damage to products or thefts. Whilst you may be very lucky and not have this happen, it is not uncommon for people to straight up steal your stuff. A good rule of thumb is the bigger the convention the more products will be damaged or go missing. Expect this. There are things you can do to mitigate some of this but be aware that this is likely to eat into your profits for the day. Also don't be afraid to speak to someone who is damaging or stealing your stuff. Sometimes people think the stuff on display is free because people are stupid and greedy. It may just be an honest mistake. But if it is not you will also find that when confronted most people will back down. Your convention may have rules in place about how they would like you to handle this. This may be a good thing to ask when you are booking your table.

Money Down

The second thing to expect is to pay to be there. Generally you have to pay to be given a space to set up. You will likely also be expected to follow very strict rules about being inside a certain space (which is usually marked on the floor) and there will be behavioural expectations as well. This will usually be located in some clandestine part of a website which will be linked or emailed to you at some stage during the preparation process. You are expected to have your own tables and stall space usually and sometimes they will even have rules about what you can and can't sell. I know one of the craft conventions I was looking to sell at pre-pandemic would not let you sell things that weren't handmade, so basically half my inventory would not have been accepted.

The Buddy System

Thirdly make sure you have a "booth buddy" to be at your booth with you. You are going to be there all day and you may need someone you can trust to look after the stall whilst you take a leak or get a drink. Also it helps to have a friend along for the ride to keep you company all day. Picking a booth buddy should be a choice about business not about friendship. You aren't just picking your pal to hang out with, you are picking an employee to help you sell. They should have reasonable people skills, be approachable and most of all confident enough to not be scared of new people when the chips are down. I would encourage you to negotiate with this person to offer some kind of payment for the day's work too. This should be fair payment and not a "mates rates" underpayment.

Be a Considerate Symbiote, Again

Once you are selling a booth at the convention there is a degree of etiquette required. Firstly etiquette towards your fellow booth owners. You are likely going to be spending a whole working day or possibly three with these people. You may also run into them again in the future. Being polite and friendly and trying to "stay in your lane" is very important to keep things on good terms. Introduce yourself and make yourself seem friendly and open to them, even if you are socially anxious and stressed. Getting off on the right foot can be a simple way to make sure things go smoothly. You don't have to become best friends, just be a polite neighbour. Also be aware of the noise and visual pollution you are putting into the air. Are you playing music or talking with your friends/customers too rowdily? Do you have obnoxious flashing lights or things that jingle or tinkle or spin constantly? Is this going to annoy the heck out of your booth neighbours? Trying to be a bit conscious of these things is important to start with. Remember the toes you step on today might be connected to the butt you have to kiss tomorrow. You never know when you might benefit from working with some of these other people again in the future. Who knows where your paths might cross and when they do you are going to want them to remember you as that person who was a nice and polite neighbour, not the person that was loud, obnoxious and kept trying to poach customers.

There is also the matter of etiquette in terms of customer interactions. Selling is service and service is selling, as a cringeworthy internet video once said. You are expected to do your best to "sell" your product but at the same time to what extent is this pushing your customers away. Some degree of selling is required to actually make a profit and this can be a fine line. I think the biggest part of this isn't what you are doing but how your customer is reacting. Be passionate about the products you have made and do try to find ways that these can suit your customers, but if they seem to withdraw from you realise you may have pushed a little too hard. It is okay to back away from a sales pitch if you think your customer is made uncomfortable by your approach. Also be aware of personal space, boundaries and to be respectful at all times. I work with a lot of older women with european heritage, as a result there are many times each week when I am talking to a colleague who constantly leans into me to talk. I do not like this, I like my space. There was one day where I had backed away from one colleague so far and ended up sitting in my chair trying to give her cues that I was not wanting to continue to talk, and she continued to get closer and closer to my face, basically breathing into my mouth. She was that close. I was arched-back in my chair away from her and she was still leaning over me talking. Not everyone is good at taking social cues, particularly us nerdy folk. This is an extreme example but just be aware that if you move towards someone and they move away from you they may not want to be that close.

Power Suits and Shoulder Pads

There are many power dynamics at play and being aware of your impact on others is a good first step. Consider if you are male or female, are you friendly or stern, large stature or small statured, loud or soft speaking, do you suffer from "resting bitch/ grumpy face" like me or the opposite? Consider how all of this might cause a problem with those you are trying to sell with and try to be less of a problem. I used to work at a go kart track and we had one girl working behind the counter who was very physical and liked to touch customers as she talked. Often we had many regulars who would wait until she was busy to approach the counter for their drinks or tickets or whatever because this made them feel uncomfortable. Being aware of such things is just a personal awareness issue, and every single customer will have different tolerances for all kinds of things, be it sales, physical closeness, cringey jokes or even body odour. Whilst you can't be the perfect assistant for every customer you can be aware of the impact you are making and read social cues. More often than not being aware of social cues can help you make a greater sale. One time whilst helping at a convention stall we even had customers return just because they knew it was a safe place to stand without getting hassled, and as a result just by being there they ended up buying more stuff anyway.

Price Tags Increase Sales

Finally make sure you have clear labelling on your stall. There are so many times where I have gone to a convention as a customer and not had enough money for something I thought was really cool. Often I will grab a business card or something and get in contact once my next payday comes around. Being at a convention is often expensive. Food, events, shopping, possibly travel and hotels. It all eats into your budget. Many potential customers may just simply not have the expendable cash at that very moment. But if you clearly label where they can go to get your stuff in future this can help. Also don't be afraid to ask people to sign up to a newsletter or follow on facebook or something to get them to remember to come back looking for you. Finally putting your price on things is going to increase sales. I know this as both a customer and a seller. I have lost track of the number of times that as a seller at other peoples booths, I have been asked what the price is on something only to have the customer realise it's way cheaper than they were expecting. As a buyer I often have this problem. I don't want to seem like a tight arse so as such often won't ask how much something is, and just assume it is out of my budget. It is often the case that later on I discover that actually it was well in my price range and could have bought one. The opposite is also true. There is nothing more heartbreaking than assuming something is going to be in your budget only to get to the check out and realise there goes the pizza money and now you have no more shopping. This is often the case when I am shopping with my wife and she wants something. Of course being a caring husband I encourage her to get the things that make her happy only to later discover all our money is now gone. Clearly labelled prices help with this. I consider this good business practice in general.

Activity: Looking into Conventions

Take some time to do some research and identify conventions, events or markets local to you. Browse the website or get in contact with the organisers and see what is required to get involved. If you plan to run events one day see if you can talk to someone who has run events there before, if you plan to sell at a market stall one day see what rules there are and the costs. If you can, go as a customer/player and don't be afraid to ask questions of the people working there. If you know someone who does go to conventions or markets see if you can offer to help for the day and be their booth buddy to "learn the ropes" as it were.

Chapter 9 - Crowdfunding

No worries, I hear you say, these days Kickstarter and other crowdfunding exists. I'll just raise my cash with pre-orders from Kickstarter or whatever. Well I don't think that in this day and age it is possible to make a book about making a project without addressing crowdfunding so here we go. Strap yourselves in kids because this is a wild ride.

How Kickstarter/Crowdfunding Works

To understand what I am about to say it is imperative that we have a fundamental understanding of how most crowdfunding works. Keep in mind that different platforms can have different rules and circumstances, but generally speaking the way things work are more or less the same across most major services.

First of all, most sites require your project to be "accepted" before it can be publicly listed. Being accepted usually is about making sure you are following the platform's legal guidelines, providing true and honest information, and that what you are promising to deliver seems reasonable. A big part of this is verifying the identity of the individual who will be the contact person for the project. On the major websites about 20% of projects get rejected either for not following the rules or not being legit. Part of this step is also setting clear expectations and on many platforms this includes your "target" of how much you want to raise.

Assuming your project is accepted, your fundraising goal is set in stone from that point on. For most of the big players it then becomes a matter of sink or swim. If you make that goal then hunky dory you get the cash and can make your product. But if you are 20c short of the goal, tough luck champion, your campaign failed and you get the knowledge of knowing you wasted all your time and energy for nothing. In theory a failed goal that is high enough demonstrates that there is a potential market for the product, but just not one that is as big as you were hoping for.

This means that there is a strategy required for learning to set a goal that is low enough to get over the line. Easy, I can already hear you crying from your homes, just set it as low as possible and it will be guaranteed to pass. That's a great idea, except for the fact that you have to actually fulfil your product orders. If you don't set it high enough to include everything that is needed then that additional cost is 100% on you chucklehead. If you only charged $10 for a product and it costs $25 to make, print, ship, send secondaries from where your shipping got lost on the way, pay your writers and artists and buy isbns and all that jazz, then congrats you are now a bankrupt individual because all that extra money comes from your pocket. So you have to set it high enough to pay everyone, get printed, have a little just in case something goes wrong, and then some left over for yourself after all is said and done.

Kickstarting/Crowdfunding seems great in theory but in practice there are so many amazing loopholes and dramas with it that it really comes down to a personal choice if it is worth your time or not. To add salt into an already bitter wound, back when Kickstarter and Indigogo first came out they were designed and mostly used by indy creators who couldn't compete with the big guys, however, now the big guys are on there as well and you are still competing with them. It is a market that has become homogenised and exploited by big business in the same way that the traditional methods of funding always have been. Causing more grief is that on the lower end of the scale where creators like you and I sit, there is a plethora of projects flooding the market in constant waves making it hard to get attention. If you are just another adventure writer or fantasy novelist you are one amongst tens of thousands of projects. These days you'd also be up against the likes of Brandon Sanderson, who hardly needs a Kickstarter to launch his stuff. At this very minute there are just short of 60,000 projects trying to be backed in the publishing category alone.

And all of this is just the idea of getting noticed, we haven't even begun to talk about the hiccups with what can go wrong once you actually get successfully backed. Failure to fulfil is a serious issue and one that the courts around the world have decided to not take lightly. Kickstarter and other platforms clearly state that the risk is all on the company making the product and not on them as distributors. If a project doesn't fulfil successfully then it is on the creator to refund, not the distributor. In 2012 a board game company successfully funded a campaign for $35,000 USD to make their game "The Doom That Came To Atlantic City." After a year of trying to develop the project it became clear that their numbers didn't add up and they couldn't afford to fulfil their consignments. They canned the game and stated that they would "eventually try to give everyone a refund." The problem is that the money had already been spent and they did not have the liquid cash to send back to folks. They had a half finished product and a bunch of excuses. The creator was taken to court as an individual, and the American Federal Trade Commission ordered the creator to personally pay back over $110,000 USD to the people who funded them. This is one of several cases around the world where the courts just simply do not care about your woes. If you have taken money then you have to deliver the goods or refund it.

I personally have been a customer on several kickstarters that have gone through hell and back. I pledged to one comic campaign that had their entire shipment of printing get loaded into a container that got put on the wrong boat and when that shipping container wasn't claimed it was auctioned off in whatever country it ended up in. The comic artist then ordered a second shipment, and the boat carrying that shipment struck a reef in a one in a million storm and sank to the bottom of the pacific. As we sit here writing this today the third shipment has made it safe to the artist and is slowly getting sent out to us backers. But imagine for a second that you are that artist. All of the profit they had thought they were making from that shipment is gone and probably then some extra. How terrifying. Whilst this is absolutely an extreme example, I am yet to personally back a kickstarter (other than my own) that didn't at some point have an issue getting the product to me. My wife jokes at how me backing a project curses it to failure, but I honestly wonder if there are statistics somewhere of how many projects run into troubles after that green bar reaches 100%.

Activity - Crowdfunding Mentor
If possible try to find a creator you know that has successfully funded a crowdfunding campaign before. Ask them questions about their experience and ask them to walk you through the process they took from start to finish. If they are planning to do another crowdfunding campaign, ask them if you can shadow them through the major beats and follow along behind the scenes. They might say no, and that is okay, but if you do get this opportunity it will give you an experience well beyond anything you can read or learn online.

No Crowd, No Fund

First and foremost, and this is 100% my honest core belief regarding crowdfunding, if you have a crowd big enough to fund the project on any crowdfunding platform, then surely you have a crowd big enough to fund your project without a platform like that. Whilst it is true that some of us see the big crowdfunding giants as places to browse and support games, the bulk of us come to these projects via other means of promotion. I have never backed a Kickstarter, Indigogo, Gofundme, etc. campaign that I came across on the website of the crowdfunding platform itself. I have always found the projects that I have backed via some other means, maybe social media or guest stars on podcasts or just because I follow the creator already. Chances are that most of your projects on these platforms are going to be backed mostly by fans who already support you in other places. There is no secret kabal hiding in the shadows waiting to fund underproduced kick starters out of the good of their own hearts.

When we made our kickstarter for *Extraordinary Expeditions,* the folks over at Crit Academy and I were very nervous about breaking through that 100% mark. Even with our combined fan bases, all 17,000 followers of The Stash and 11,000 followers of Crit Academy, we only got 350 backers to fork out the funds. We made it with 135% of our goal, which was set as low as it was possible to still make a profit to split between all parties involved. Since then we have sold dozens more copies and every month more copies sneak off the shelves.

If you do not have a crowd who is willing to back you, then you don't have a crowdfund from which to get your product off the ground. If you do have a crowd of loyal followers keen to pay for your work, why are you adding a middleman? There isn't a magical audience living inside the big crowdfunding websites just waiting to make you a millionaire. Sure you may get a few extra sales but no more than if you were to spend the same amount of time and energy and stress that is required to successfully launch on one of these platforms instead doing some marketing and getting booked on podcasts and vlogs and review channels on YouTube. No crowd, no fund!

Fulfilment Breaks the Bank

The next big hurdle comes if you do get funded. Books have to be printed. Writers have to be paid. Art has to be bought. Layout and editing has to be sourced. Shipments have to be made at all stages, between the printers and the creators, the creators and the distributors, the distributors to the customer. A physical print of a book from a crowdfunded project will potentially be triple or double handled, with a cost for moving that physical product at every stage. If something isn't right with the print sample then this can add extra costs to make the required changes. If something goes wrong with any of those shipments, and in my experience as a customer it certainly does so regularly, then that adds to the cost. There are a lot of extra parts in a machine that could be much simpler. Compare all that to a simple print on demand service where once the book is made it is shipped directly to the customer from the printer. By removing all the additional parts that are involved in bulk printing and distribution suddenly you have a lot less potential for things to go horribly wrong. Regardless of which method you choose to pursue, the key thing to note is that there are production costs beyond just getting the book printed. In a crowdfunding environment you often must calculate your costs ahead of time to set your goal in the first place.

Often new crowdfunding creators fail to crunch all these numbers in their budget when they first submit it to their platform for approval. In other cases, in order to keep that target as low as possible to ensure that they can actually reach it with their smaller fan base the creators forget or choose not to include a large enough buffer for issues that may arise. This can cripple a company trying to fulfil its consignments through crowdfunding.

A very common mistake that I hear about is stretch goals and how they impact production costs. Sure when you were making a simple 64 page softcover book your numbers worked out just fine and dandy. However in order to entice customers some creators offer very extensive stretch goals. "For an extra $1,000 we will add ten new class archetypes! At $2,000 five new dungeons or at $3,000 a hardcover." All of a sudden those class archetypes are adding twenty pages to your book. Those five dungeons which got you to the two grand mark just added an additional fifteen to twenty pages. Now your book is an optimistic 100 pages, which in most printers is double or more the print cost. Not to mention that your hardcover option usually multiplies that once more by at least 150%. Now let us not forget that you have just added thirty five to forty pages of content, which means you will need to pay for it to be written, for any art, for it to be edited, and for those pages to be added to the layout costs. Even ignoring printing costs this makes a huge dent in your profits. If that $1,000 lot you just pulled out of your butt is split over 300 backers, you have just gone into the red on designing and printing this project.

What you also forget to realise was that you also just added twice as much weight for shipping. Now some crowdfunding projects do not include shipping, but I can tell you when I am a customer and the shipping is more than the product I tend to get a bit upset. This often happens to me because I live in Australia. It then makes me not want to keep supporting those creators because I got screwed on shipping.

Fulfilment of your promises is often the element that messes up the maths for many creators and it is quite common to hear these horror stories when you are talking with people behind the scenes. Many mentors, coaches and crowdfunding managers will tell you that making sure you crunch the numbers correctly is the most important thing you can do. My tip if you do decide to head down this route is to always underpromise and overdeliver. It is better to promise four stretch levels each adding one bonus, than offering one level at four times the cost that promises four bonuses. If your followers really want all that extra content then they will be willing to add onto the stretch goals.

Activity - Research Failed Crowdfunding Fulfilments
There are many famous cases of failed crowdfunding fulfillments. If you do plan to go down the route of crowdfunding, please take a few hours to go down a rabbithole and research some of the more notable failures in fulfilments. This is not something I want you to do because I am trying to scare you off, but because if you learn from their mistakes then you are more likely to not make that same mistake. Stephen King often says he would rather read 100 trashy, badly written stories, than one single well written masterpiece because he knows he will learn so much more from the badly written dumpster fire of a book than he ever will from something that is perfect. You should be the same when considering something as serious as pursuing large sums of money.

Money Now, Product Now

Again we see the shifting nature of crowdfunding manipulate and contort the original intention of the beast. When crowdfunding first started with platforms like Kickstarter and Indigogo being for the independent creators there was an understanding that pledging to support a campaign was a preorder. It was for creators who had no way of raising the kinds of funds needed to hire writers, artists, editors and layout designers. It was a way for creators to buy the raw materials to build the content they needed to create. Rather than take out a bank loan or hit up their families and friends for money they would ask the audience to pay ahead of time and that would give them the investment they needed to get on their feet and get the project made. These days this is no longer the case.

With the interference of big business getting involved on crowdfunding platforms, the business model of "we have a product ready to go, would you like to preorder it and we can ship it right away" has swiftly become the expectation of many backers online. Many of the creators I have spoken to who have successfully crowdfunded projects have all had one big piece of feedback for me, and that is that customers expect the product to be ready right away. I have been told by no less than twelve creators that if I want to crowdfund a project I better have all the writing done before I even think about submitting a proposal to the platform because once the bidding war starts there is an expectation that the product is in the hands of the consumer with as minimal turn around as is possible.

This obviously shifts a lot of the balance from the original intention of these platforms away from indy friendly content creators. This is not because of any decisions that the platforms have made, but instead just how the market has come to expect a certain level of speed due to the whales in the koi pond. Whilst this does cause a problem, there is no real solution now that we are so deep into the culture of crowdfunding. Be aware of this expectation.

I can't help but wonder if this expectation is actually a manifestation of anxiety over how many of these crowdfunded projects do become horror shows, or at least the perception that tragedy could happen to any project that has been backed and that money lost to the consumer. Maybe it is just a community of eager gamers who are not used to delayed gratification. Either way they have paid their money and they want their product yesterday. So be ready for that as a creator.

Activity - Task Priority Based Project Management
If you are considering undertaking a project that you would like to fund through a crowdfunding platform, make a list of every step that will be required. Writing each chapter, editing

each chapter, locating art, playtesting, getting layout done, sample printing, etc. Once you have this list, mark next to each section anything that can be done before your campaign gets submitted. Is it possible to get everything written, or do you need the money for that? Is it possible to get some editors or playtesters who can play an unedited version? Can you shortlist the art you want to buy ahead of time and make a temporary shopping list so that when the green light gets funded you can just click "go to checkout" and be 100% ready to get the show on the road as swiftly as possible. If you plan to successfully get the tasks done anyway, this kind of task focussed project management is going to be required regardless. If you can prioritise the tasks that are most urgent and can be done ahead of time you may make a workflow that is entirely efficient for future use regardless of whether you crowdfund or not.

Additionally do some research into Task Priority Project Management and learn how the real professional project managers do their thing. This can be a valuable skill for life let alone business and has the potential to change your outlook on the entire world.

Chapter 10 - Fiction Writing

What is gamemastering if not just writing fiction? One of my favourite memes is a screen capture of a twitter user saying "I want to GM my own game, play all the NPCs and all the characters." and then a reply saying "People are telling me this is called 'writing a book'." I honestly cannot think of a more apt way of describing how fiction writing can be approached by an experienced game master. There are a few subtle differences which we can discuss here.

I feel that all the methods before this point, with the exception of adventure writing, have been asking game masters to locate other areas of skill and learn how to add them to their toolset. Performing on camera or microphone, negotiating a convention table of strangers, becoming retail experts at random craft markets and conventions. It is all a bit of a stretch from where our real skill set lies. At our heart, us game masters are storytellers and crafters of plot. Fiction writing seems like a natural next step for many of us and often this is because we want to use the stories and worlds we have created in our impromptu games.

I find the problem with this approach lies in the differentiation between what works in a roleplaying game and what works in fiction writing. Whilst I have no doubt in your ability to craft an amazing story for players of your roleplaying game, writing fiction is a different beast. Not only do you need to have a great plot and characters but actually be able to craft paragraphs to create the artistry you want. Writing is something many people think they do well but actually can't see they are flawed at. This shouldn't be disparaging because being aware of the common mistakes is a great way to transition from gaming into fiction. Aside from being a hobby that I am far too fussy about, I put myself through some great expense to add a major of literature and creative writing to my otherwise unrelated degree. This eventually was the major that I used to weasel my way into teaching English and now I get to teach how to write fiction well on a daily basis. I also get to read lots of not so great writing and help the writers become stronger and better. Watching that journey is one of my favourite parts of my job. We always put fiction in Dice Ranger Magazine because I love seeing new writers get a chance to get their work out there in the world.

As an aside if you are an aspiring fiction writer, then this is exactly the kind of people Arjade Productions is looking for and you should definitely reach out to us if you would like to write some fiction for us. I am happy to help guide writers of any experience level to find ways to improve. We are also always looking for reliable writers to add to our list.

Storytelling vs Fiction Writing

The kind of writing I am doing here is absolutely not the kind of writing I do for fiction. This book is fast and loose and mostly just me imparting key pieces of my story to you. Likewise, the kind of storytelling I do when I am game mastering is similarly sloppy. I take all the low hanging fruit, manipulate emotions with it, develop characters of both the non-player and player variety way faster and with less sincerity than I ever would putting real pen to page for something I wanted to publish. Fiction writing is quite literally an art form. Whether it is short stories, novels or something else entirely it requires a great deal of artistic consideration and structure to pull off well.

Each form of fiction has its own challenges and structures and this, like most of my advice in this book, is not really something we are going to get into in depth here. Maybe one day I will publish a book on how to write fiction of various kinds, and if that is something you would be interested in purchasing let me know so that I can bump it up the priority list. The key information here is understanding how to wield those weapons is a skill that must be learned before you can successfully make money at it. Think of storytelling like a longsword. It is straight and easy to use without causing too much of a problem. Most people can grab a longsword and attack someone with it and for the most part use it without too much drama. But fiction writing is more like fighting with nunchucks. When it is done correctly it looks really cool and effortless and most people think it is easy. However, after grabbing a set and giving it a few swirls the wielder almost always hurts themselves in a way that makes them look particularly foolish.

If you are already a game master then you will have a great deal of skill working with characters and plot. This is an asset that many have to work hard to learn. This is a skill that is very difficult to teach but absolutely essential to skillful writing. You are already quite capable of such a thing if you can consistently keep four to eight players intrigued at the hot air vibrating out your mouth for hours at a time. Often a great game master will understand the subtleties of motivation, complication, climax and balanced rewards. They will understand power and when to overwhelm the protagonists with it and when to balance it evenly. They will understand the dynamics of people with different motivations and how to find ways to push those divides whilst not breaking the relationships. Game masters are outstanding storytellers and are often more than half way on the journey to becoming great fiction writers.

Game Mastering Plus Art Equals Fiction

Fiction writing requires patience and planning. The incorporation of aspects like theme and extended metaphor are also required to make something really pop. Knowing what to show the audience and what not to show them is a skill, all with the aim of giving them just enough information to piece it together without having to tell them what is going on. Knowing how to focus a story through the correct character so as not to reveal too much or too little is a skill. All of these skills that must be learnt on top of actually writing something artistic and interesting. Writing metaphors in a way that isn't clumsy or cliched. Describing a scene in a way that evokes a clear image in the reader's mind without making reference to another image by saying things such as "it's like that one castle in skyrim where there is like this mountain and a bunch of caves and the ramp leading up to it." We might do this in a game master setting but not in fiction writing. Fiction writing is a thoughtful process, and is often solitary in nature. Actions of characters are uninspired by the randomness of what others are thinking and interpreting. Whilst it is theoretically true that one could turn the stories from roleplaying game sessions into fiction, it is often the case that those stories actually do not make that great a fiction at all. Often the storylines and characterisations are rather derivative and far too tropey for successful narrative in a modern audience.

The first step to making money as a game master turned fiction writer is to understand the significant differences between publishable fiction and just throwing a bunch of characters into a dungeon to fight some kobolds. Once you can master those differences you will make stories that fans will love and be immersed whole heartedly into, however this will take some practising and often require you to write some pretty garbage stuff for a bit until you find your feet.

Editing is Key

90% of great fiction writing is actually fixing badly written fiction. No story is perfect on its first burst out from your brain. They say that the goal of the first draft is to be written on the page. The goal of the second draft is to be as completely different from the first draft as is possible whilst still retaining the story. The truth is that even the best writers write like crap the first time around. You have to edit your work thoroughly. This often means rewriting whole chunks of story to make things fit how they are supposed to.

This is simultaneously liberating and entirely frustrating at the same time. The benefit of this is that you absolutely can be confident in writing your first draft knowing that it is just fine the way it is. Just write it. Put one word; and then another; and then some more until you have a completed first draft. Don't even think about it. You don't even need to read it as you go if you don't want to. Just get it written. This is the biggest hurdle. With the advent of google drives and mobile phones we can be adding bits of writing to our first draft anywhere we want. You could even be writing your first draft on the toilet. If crap is coming out one end already, why not have it go both ways? Get the first draft complete and do not think twice about whether it is good or bad. Every first draft is perfect as a first draft, except the first draft that is incomplete. The frustrating bit comes at the second draft.

Second Draft Stutters

Once the first draft is done, entirely free from any constraints imposed by thoughts of perfection, skill or artistry we must then reframe our mind to start adding those criticisms. The second draft is the first edit. Editing is where real stories are made. Many game masters struggle with this aspect of the writing process. We are so used to just running a game session once and taking what we have and working with it. We are very flexible when it comes to bad storytelling or lack of artistry. Once you can overcome this fear you will start to become not just a better fiction writer, but also a better game master.

Revisiting a story is not a criticism of that story. Every story can be revisited and improved. You are not a failure if you have to return to a story and make changes that improve it. Once you begin to do this for fiction writing you will actually learn many things about how to tell a story better in the first draft. This is a skill that directly translates across to game mastering. Embracing this mindset is going to make you a better storyteller in the long run.

The actual process of how to edit is also something that many beginners struggle with. Most people think "editing, it's just checking spelling and grammar right?" but actually that is the last step of editing that you should do. Your first edit and therefore subsequent second draft should actually be looking at things like story beats, overarching plot structures, characterisation, timeline issues, if your narrator is the correct one for the scene, and other really major changes to the story. If you do the second draft correctly you will likely edit in and out whole massive chunks of text. Sometimes adding whole pages of content. Following rounds of editing and drafting are going to be doing the opposite of that, tearing out whole chunks of text to cut your story down to its most minimal effective product. Finally you are going to want to do some editing passes where you deliberately go in and focus just on individual things, such as dialogue, artistry, description, foreshadowing and theme. Again adding and removing as required.

Only after you have done all this should you actually do a final pass to look at spelling, grammar, and punctuation. The reason for this is that if you did that basic editing pass at the start, you would be wasting so much time. Think about it, if you spend hours reading and rewriting whole sections of your book only to add to it and then tear bits out again and again, how many times are you going to be going back to correct grammar? Two, three, seven? Who is to say? If you ignore it until the end you only need to correct errors like that once. I know this feels weird but trust me, it saves you hours and hours in the long run.

There are plenty of YouTube videos, blog posts and whole books out there that explain how to write and edit a work of fiction. Go and seek them out.

Activity - Write Your First Draft Unapologetically
For this activity I want you to just get started on writing a draft for a work of fiction. If this is the path you have chosen, just do it. I mean, it can't be worse than many of the "classics" that are out there. Have you actually read the classics? As an English teacher my students for whom English is an additional language often ask me if reading books like Frankenstein, Gulliver's Travels, or Shakespeare are good things for them to read. I alway have to try to convince them that, actually, all of the "classics" written hundreds of years ago are actually badly written by today's standards of english. Languages evolve, and so too do what readers expect in a story. If you are expecting to write fantasy fiction the same way Tolkien did, or heck, even R.A. Salvatore, or Weis and Hickman, wrote just a few decades ago, you are sorely mistaken. Writing has moved on from those basic levels of storytelling and if you want to be successful you will also have to improve beyond that. But not in your first

draft. Your first draft is a) absolutely going to be better than the three greats mentioned above (Jonathan Swift couldn't even learn when to capitalise a letter for crying out loud) and b) doesn't have to be perfect. It just has to be written. So the activity for this chapter is simple, write your damn first draft already. Stop making excuses.

Activity - Submit a Short Story
The other side of writing is submitting stories. Many people are scared of being rejected when they submit their stories. Overcoming this is a very crucial part of being a writer. Whether you plan to self publish or submit to a "proper" publishing house in the traditional way, you are going to at some point have to show your work to someone. So let me make this easy for you. Submit a short story to Dice Ranger Magazine. You can find details for how to do that in the magazine itself, available from Arjade.net. We pay for every story published and as long as a story is short enough to fit into the issue, doesn't contain any material that would cause us concern (we try to keep it PG and inclusive where possible) and is appropriate for the content of the issue, we generally publish it. There have been some times where we have worked with the writer to make some minor improvements, but that story after one or two revisions is usually published and paid for. So, if you are reading this, send us a story and overcome your fear of submitting work. The goal of Arjade Productions is to publish new authors of all kinds and one day we hope to be large enough to make that happen on a large scale, but for now we have a small magazine and you are welcome to publish with us to break your fear of submission. Alternatively submit to anywhere you think appropriate. The key takeaway is just to submit something.

Marketing

Now we get to the pointy end of this method. Whether you plan to submit to a traditional publishing house or self publish, at some point you are going to have to market your book. It is very possible to make a living off publishing books, even self published ones, however these days if you are going to do that you will need to learn how to market your work. A large part of this at the time of writing this book is the incorporation of a social media strategy. There are whole YouTube channels, Instagram accounts, and blog posts dedicated to teaching you how to do this. There are also many paid courses that can assist with this. I highly recommend that you find a reputable guide in your price range (prices range from free on YouTube to costing thousands for a mentor to provide one-on-one tuition) and learn how to market your books.

It is absolutely possible to make money with the creative skills you learnt as a game master by utilising them to write fiction. Unfortunately learning marketing is a step that you must learn if you do want to make money doing this in the long term.

Activity - Find Some Role Models

Go onto instagram, facebook, YouTube or twitter and find some authors whom you appreciate the work of. See how they market themselves. Make a note of what kinds of content they post, how regularly they post, if there is a pattern to their posting schedule or content and if any of these ideas inspire you for your own author page. Notice how many of them make content other than just about pushing their books onto people. Take a note of how they approach the posts where they do try to sell their books. Are these sales creating effective engagement or are they outliers in an otherwise well interacted with account? The best way to start to understand what is required of you as an author in the marketing landscape is to simply study what other people are doing and try to find your own way of doing that.

Chapter 11 - Content Writing and Copywriting

Fiction writing isn't the only way to make money writing these days. In fact there are so many opportunities to get paid for writing. Blogs, websites, YouTubers, reviewers, podcasts and online stores all need content written for them. It is its own sub-industry and one that can be incredibly profitable. Getting into this kind of writing might seem like a big jump from running a roleplaying game, but at the end of the day you are a storyteller and so much of what is needed these days is that gift.

Writing is Writing

One of the jokes I hear again and again is about how when you want to look up a recipe these days first you have to hear about how the writer of the recipe once rode their bicycle to their grandmothers house on an autumn day through a bunch of orange maple leaves and the smell of that maple forest always reminded them of their grandmothers love and so making these pancakes is going to warm your heart and soul not just your belly. See, even in that little reference you can see the power of just telling a little story, but my point is that so much of today's content is just churned out hand over fist. It is seen as disposable content, pumped and dumped. Despite this, it is still required to make some kind of emotional connection to keep people on the page.

Whether it is a random core memory from a food blogger or a review of the latest tech gadget or the copy for the pair of earrings being imported from AliExpress by some dropshipper, all of these written word articles need some kind of lengthy writing to justify the SEO on their pages and "produce content" to be consumed. Many of these jobs are farmed out to contractors. Taking a look on Fiverr, there are over 15,000 content writing jobs currently being advertised. These are all people who are making money from paid writing gigs. You could easily become one of the many who are doing this. The fact so many exist on a single site is because there is a key market out there for this kind of work. If you are creative you too can also find success with this.

Now, I just referenced Fiverr because it is one of the leading sources of getting workers for this kind of job, though let it be known that getting a job on this site will often be low paying and fairly boring kinds of stuff. That is not to say that you can't make yourself a successful content writing or copywriting business.

Copywriting vs Content Writing

Copywriting (writing product page descriptions and marketing materials) is probably one of the biggest writing industries for online content creators. The reason for this is because without good copy, products do not sell. Getting good at this often requires learning some skills and rules but once you wrap your head around those the key to success is usually about being able to weave a good story that demonstrates the need for a product that otherwise seems pointless. Often these stories are told in a second person format, which is handily the same kind of narrative structure that a game of dungeons and dragons is told in. As game masters we are skilled at manipulating the emotions of our players and really deep down at its core this is all copywriting is.

Content writing is where you are writing articles and content for blogs or general interest websites. There was a time where I had quit teaching temporarily and the ghostwriting I did on the side as a content writer made me enough money to pay some of our bills. What was my key to success? Weaving an engaging and emotional narrative. A lot of the content I was writing was in the sphere of computer/video gaming and trying to draw people into the emotional state of mind that they fall into when they play those games was a skill that I developed very quickly. It is perfect for game masters like us who thrive on seeing threads of emotionally viable narrative and pulling them until our audience is putty in our hands.

In both of the aforementioned fields, copywriting and content writing, you will have to learn to write efficiently and within parameters given to you in a brief. Aside from that there is little difference in writing that kind of content or social media posts, dungeon delving adventures or narrative fiction. The core of it all is remembering that you are writing for a human on the other end of the words and finding ways to manipulate that can be very skillful indeed.

If this is something you are interested in doing there are once again thousands of tutorials, courses and programs you can join to teach you the skills required to do this. Go out and learn what needs to be done and you never know, you might find not just a new side hustle, but potentially a new career. It will also help you write your own content and copy if you do try to sell your own goods in some fashion, be it dungeon adventures, fantasy fiction or even just selling your services as a gamemaster.

Activity - Building a Portfolio
Pick 20 products that you like and use. Try to pick a range of products, not just ten of the same thing. Try to vary the price, size, purpose and usefulness of the products as much as possible. Maybe you choose your computer monitor, your dishwasher, your car, your favourite kind of pen, your favourite brand of energy drink, your cats favourite brand of food, your toothpaste, your favourite movie, and so on. Once you have that list, go online and see what the current copy for selling this product is in a variety of places; maybe the supermarket, and the actual official webpage and maybe some instagram posts. After you get a feel for how that product is currently advertised write four original pieces of content/copy for that product in a similar style to that which you have seen advertised. That is not to say copy what is there, but try to write something that sells the product. Writing an Instagram Caption, a Webstore Page, a Podcast Advert Script, and a Product Review for each product will give you a good feel for how you can sell things in different formats. Try to use your ability to impact an audience here. How can you create an emotional connection? How can you use that connection to sell the product?

If you have done this for twenty products you should have a pretty solid portfolio to get feedback on. If possible, reach out to someone who is currently already doing copywriting and ask them if they could give you feedback on your work. Make the changes they have suggested and see if you can learn why those changes needed to be made. Get multiple opinions on this if possible. Once multiple people say your writing is ready, see if you can find somewhere to get hired.

Out of the Box

You might be very surprised by just how many jobs exist out there for a skillful writer who can manipulate an audience. Think of the content you consume, who is writing that? Tiktok posts, Instagram captions, recipes, blogs, tweetstorms, heck even just the twitter of most celebrities is all written by someone else. See how much of this is writing that you could be doing. Writing jokes for webcomics, hell even making an indy comic script and getting it turned into a proper comic is an avenue for using these skills. The key here is to trying to find ways to use your gift at storytelling to get you into a position to charge for that writing.

When I was younger I worked at a go-kart track, but the way I got that job was by writing a somewhat creative cover letter for my resume. I had been out of work for a while and instead of just writing a traditional "I want to work for you because, and here is my experience" cover letter I took a risk and after the first two introductory, stereotypical paragraphs I instead began to weave a story about my situation. I explained how my resume looked somewhat stark in the six months previous to the application, having not worked for the bulk of that time. I explained that I had been ill, but that had not impacted my work ethic. I sold the story of me, a young man who wanted to find a way out of a rut and was looking for a chance to find an organisation where he could make his triumphant and dedicated return to the workforce. I detailed that I had been spending the past six months teaching myself many skills in my home, including graphic design and website editing, skills that I could take to whatever company offered me the opportunity to get back on my feet. I appealed to their reputation as a community fixture and wove in a story about how my friends and I went there as teens. When I was offered the interview the process went very smoothly because they felt like they knew a chunk of my story already. It turned out that they were actually looking for someone who was tech savvy because they were really not very good with that stuff. If I hadn't gone out on a limb and tried a narrative approach I would probably not have received the job. From there I got to work making promotional materials for them, just flyers and stuff. I also made an excel program to help their less math-capable employees how to add up the till at the end of the shift. Both of these things I used in my portfolio when applying for other jobs, again getting me work in various retail positions later on in my working life.

Sometimes thinking in a creative way can get you somewhere you didn't think you wanted to be, but at the end of the day it might just take you to a place where you learn a skill you never knew you needed. One of my favourite books is Freakonomics and I highly recommend you have a read of it, no matter what you plan to do with your life. The stories in that book help you to look at life in a very different way. If you are planning to do any kind of content or copywriting then asking questions that really take you to interesting places is only going to help improve the results that you get.

Diversity of Product

As I write this book our global economy is about to go into a recession. Michael Burry, the guy who predicted the 2008 Global Financial Crisis and profited from it, has just gone on the record saying that later this year (2022) is going to be an even bigger plane crash for the world's economy. We are in a perfect storm of bad finances worldwide. Part of this is due to the global pandemic and governments responses (or lack of response) to that. Part of this is that wage growth has stagnated over the past decade and is at record lows. Workers everywhere are refusing to tolerate the bad treatment that has been going on since I entered the workforce almost 20 years ago and the loose cash people have to spend is disappearing as we all tighten our belt straps.

When funds get tight, one of the first markets to take a toll is the hobby industry. People need food, clothes, petrol and transport. What they don't need is plastic dolls in the shape of an orc and some book telling them how to pretend to find treasure in a crypt filled with undead. If you are putting all your eggs in that one basket you are going to have a bad time. This is generally good advice, diversifying your products leads to more safety as a creator, but in a time of financial crisis and when your niche is an industry that is a luxury that many can't afford, that advice should ring loud and clear like a bell.

If you are seeking to be a content creator of any kind, diversifying your products is going to give you a life raft to float on. If you can find ways into avenues other than gaming content you are going to be able to be agile, reactive and adaptive. Three features which will provide you with longevity in your career. Maybe you don't go into copywriting or content writing, but looking for other avenues of income is definitely a good idea in a time like today. The wider you cast your net the more kinds of fish you will be likely to catch. I wish you luck with whatever you end up doing and if you come up with any cool ideas because of this book please let me know.

Chapter 12 - Products Multiplied by Time Equals Profit

Okay, we are now in our final official chapter. Regardless of what pathway you have chosen, however many chapters you totally skipped over, this chapter is the final key piece of advice everyone should know. The real formula for success here isn't any one activity. It's that with products and services on the shelf, and the persistence to keep offering those products and services over time you will inevitably at some point start to make a move towards profit if you continue to give energy to that pursuit. That last one was a very long sentence so let's simplify it. More products equals more potential for sales each day, more days equals more profits. The more products you have the more money you can make. Also the more time each individual product is on the market, the more money it will make for you. Products x Time = Profit.

Your Biggest Ally

Your biggest ally in all of this is time. The sooner you start creating products and promoting them, the sooner you will have built a catalogue of products. With an ever growing catalogue of both evergreen and trending products being promoted over time you will see some kind of success.

Nothing here is a get-rich-quick scheme. Every avenue that is there to be taken will slowly grow into something if you continue to nurture it and nourish it and give it some energy. When I started at Game Master Stash we had under 1,000 followers. And all I and the other admins did was post every day one simple post. We didn't buy advertising. We didn't push or promote the page. All we did was make daily content and then out of nowhere one of us realised "Hey admins, did you realise we are coming up on 12,000 followers. We should probably do something to celebrate that!" And then just months after that the figure had grown to 17,000. All we did was post regularly and occasionally reply to comments. As you grow you eventually reach a critical mass where the growth happens without you trying. Just focus on creating regular content and over time those numbers add up.

Likewise when I first published my very first module for Pathfinder in 2018 I made a few dozen sales in that first year. Now as I write this book just four years later I have had nearing 5,000 sales across my product lines. Over time these products continue to make me small amounts of money here and there. Time is the only key to this, and as more time passes you can continue to increase the number of ways to capitalise on your gifts as a game master and storyteller.

Building a Catalogue

One product over a decade will make you some money, but for every product you increase in your product line you multiply the potential earnings of your operation. This allows you to scale your business slowly, piece by piece, until eventually you have waves of income coming from a variety of sources. Time is great at multiplying money, but building out your catalogue is ultimately the best way to increase your business model. Whether it is increasing your books published, be they adventure modules or works of fiction, or producing more video or podcast episodes on to which advertising revenue can be earned, or simply just running more sessions over the course of time, your ultimate goal has to be some kind of expansion.

There are two approaches to this, the first is the casual approach as I have been doing. Simply adding a new title every year or so when you have the time to write it and get it made. This obviously is slower but is ultimately more sustainable in the long run. It allows you to have a life, a family, a career on top of making quality content. The other approach is often referred to as the "shotgun" method, one of my friends also calls this the "spaghetti at the wall" method, where you just spam a whole bunch of mediocre quality stuff and hope something sticks.

Either way, regardless of what you try, the fact that you have more products to choose from adds more potential for sales. This kind of growth has a compounding effect. Just as with time your sales grow, so too does your catalogue. Do not be afraid to add slowly piece by piece until you finally have a collection to rival even the larger game studios.

You can also diversify your products. I have done this, starting with Pathfinder and then to Call of Cthulhu modules. This allows you to tap multiple fan bases. As time goes on it is my plan to continue to develop those product lines. Not to mention the fiction that is in the works as we speak. Developing a diverse catalogue will help you stay afloat in case any one ship starts to sink. Again taking your time with this is absolutely okay. Ironically, as I write this I have planned three or four projects for 5e Dungeons and Dragons that are all in various states of production. Today they announced their new edition which will be released shortly. Imagine having twenty or thirty products all dedicated to a single edition of a game and then how the release of a new edition would impact the sales of that empire that you have built up. This is the risk you make when you specialise.

Passive Income

It is vital to have a monetisation strategy from the get go, otherwise you are not a business you are just a hobbyist. Whilst this is absolutely fine if that is what you intend to be, if your plan is for greater things then you can't start off with no plan. It is very difficult to turn a hobby into a business once you are several years down the track. The goal we are talking about here is passive income. Income that is made without you having to do anything. Consider ways you can make income off your hard work, but more than that consider ways you can reinvest that income to grow the overall potential of your business.

As mentioned above, these days I am nearing 5,000 sales of my products. I add a new product every couple of seasons. It is my goal to increase that catalogue when I get the chance, but even with my meagre amount of products every couple of months I log into my drivethrurpg account and discover enough money to buy more stock art for the next project. Or in some very rare cases enough money to pay my bills. I am not doing anything to really promote most of these products. I mostly just post a photo of them on Instagram once in a while. This income is a pleasant surprise as I am doing nothing to drive it.

As time goes on, and my catalogue increases, the payday will only continue to grow.

Having Fun

The final and most important tip here is to have fun. If it is not fun then you aren't doing it right. There are moments when it can be stressful and there are moments like right now, at 2.30am on a Friday night/Saturday morning where I am up working late into the small hours of the moon, where it is hard work. But at the end of it all, when you look at a finished product, or at your latest episode views, or when you talk to your community and they are excited to be involved with you, that is when your soul fills with joy. You made that and no one can take that away from you.

If it ever doesn't feel like that, get in touch and let me help you, because it should be fun. After all, it's just a game.

Conclusion

I couldn't believe it. I felt all giddy, like before a first date or in the car ride home after buying a brand new treat for myself that I couldn't wait to dig into. It was euphoric. It was ecstatic. I had finally done it! I couldn't believe it. I hadn't felt this good in a long time and I was high on the thrill of it. I sat and read the email for the one thousandth time in an hour.

"Congratulations, your work has been published!"

This was the moment I knew for sure that I was doing the one thing I would do until my last days on this planet. As a very small boy I had always wanted to see my name on the spine of a book, Raymond J. Hicks, and there it was! I was a published author. I knew this was only the beginning of something much greater. One day I would make my entire living from this. One day this would be what paid my bills. But right now that didn't matter because I knew this was the first step on a journey I had been preparing to take my entire life.

The next day, as I explained to my friends what I had done, I heard them respond with varying degrees of enthusiasm; some supportive, some jealous, some trying to tear me down. One thing flowed through many of their responses though. They wanted that dream too. Many of them wanted to get their work out there. I had known that for a while. It was then I realised what I really wanted. As much as publishing my own work was important to me, I had a new goal. I decided that day that what I really wanted to do with my publishing company was start helping others to find the way to reach that goal. I began to work in whatever way I could. At first just motivating and encouraging them. Where I could, I paid people to become writers or artists for me. I wanted to share my success with others.

That is what Arjade Productions is all about; building a community of people who help each other. I hope this book one day helps you to build your own empire. I absolutely believe you can do it. But first you have to take your first step. When you do, let me know so that I can buy your cool stuff too. We have to support each other.

Thank you for reading this book. Now go and make something of your own and sell it to me.

For more visit www.ARJADE.net

Made in United States
Troutdale, OR
11/03/2026

56844869R00070